Mission: Mother Earth

PEACE THROUGH GEOBIOLOGY

Richard Benishai

The use of maps in this book has been authorized
by written permission of the Survey of Israel, under license.

Library of Congress Cataloging-in-Publication Data
Benishai, Richard, 1943-
Mission: Mother Earth: peace through geobiology / Richard Benishai.
pages cm --(Between the Earth and the Skies series; book one)
Includes bibliographical references and index.
ISBN 978-0-926524-74-3 (paperback)
1.Geobiology--Philosophy. 2.Geobiology--Social aspects--Israel.
3.Peace-building--Israel. 4.Benishai, Richard--Travel--Israel. 5.Leys--Israel.
6.Israel--Description and travel. 7.Healers--Biography. 8.Channeling
(Spiritualism) 9. Extraterrestrial beings. 10.Healing--Social aspects--Israel. I.
Title. II. Title: Mother Earth.
QH343.4.B47 2013
577--dc23

Printed in the United States of America.
Address all inquiries to:
Granite Publishing
P.O. Box 1429
Columbus, NC 28722
http://granitepublishing.us

Acknowledgements

It is only through the kind services and help of
Vardit Fabran that I was able to complete this new book.
Vardit was able to turn a plain, technical rendition of my work
into an exciting and pleasing adventure into conscious development.

<u>Series</u>
Between the Earth and the Skies

<u>Book One</u>

Mission: Mother Earth

Contents

Illustrations

Prologue

Early morning, I stand facing the horizon, spread-eagled on the shore of Netanya in Israel—just like Leonardo da Vinci's famous sketch. Inhaling deeply, I gaze upon the wide open spaces—just so, I muse, might Leonardo himself have stood while doing his morning exercises.

Leonardo drew his "Vitruvius Man" sketch in *De Architectura* about 1490, in accordance with a description by the Roman architect Marcus Vitruvius of the internal proportions of the male human body. His sketch depicts a naked male figure in two superimposed positions with his arms and legs apart such that the man in the drawing has four arms and four legs. You can just picture him skipping lightly from one posture to another: Hop, two, three, four… hop, two, three, four…

Slightly short of breath after these early morning exertions, I still conjure up the Vitruvius figure that exemplifies the perfect proportions and symmetry of the human figure—just as a powerful fitness instructor might do.

The figure is simultaneously inscribed in both a circle and a square. This sketch symbolizes perfection and harmony and thus, as early as the first century BCE, Vitruvius pointed to the human form as the essential source of and inspiration for the proportions obtained in classic architecture. Leonardo sought to emphasize an even more important point concerning man's relations with the cosmos—he believed the workings of the human body to be analogous to the workings of the universe. In visual language, he shows that when a man stretches out his arms to the fullest extent, the proportions between the ends of his hands, his feet and an invisible point representing the tip of a cocked hat over his head, create a five-sided star, namely the pentagram.

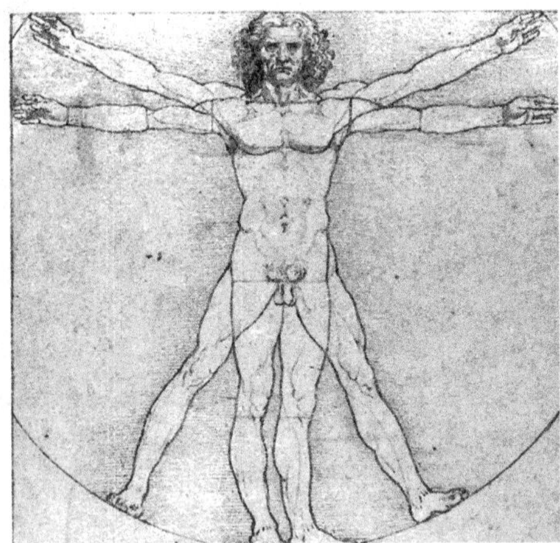

Accordingly, his sketch also symbolizes man—his feet planted on the earth (the square) while his head is in the sky (the circle). The sketch embodies both matter and spirit within itself, serving as an intermediary between the two. In the building of cathedrals, the initial dimensions of the edifice were based on the same circle-and-square combination. These two basic forms provided a spiritual connection to the Earth and the Heavens.

Still contemplating the sea, I hear the constant splash of the waves and their incessant motion. What signs and omens do I seek in the wide open space in front of me? In a world that conceals more than it reveals? Like many a mortal before me, I grasp at any manifestation that lets me catch a glimpse of some deliberate intent. This is the viewpoint of the geobiologist, as he endeavors to capture signs of the intelligence that directs the workings of the universe.

For example, consider the golden ratio on which Leonardo's teacher, Luca Pacioli wrote in the 15th century in The Divine Proportions, his book on mathematics. For many people, this golden mean became a mystic principle, expressive of the presence of the infinite in Creation and manifesting itself in the physical dimension. This wondrous proportion can be found everywhere. Nature shows it in diverse forms—in shells, in flowers and so forth.

Mathematicians call it phi, an irrational number starting with 1.618. The ongoing digits after the decimal point create an infinite string of numbers, like a long tail that keeps extending into the depths of the mysterious outer reaches of the universe. Some refer to it as the signature of the Creator. Certain singularly favored individuals since the dawn of human civilization have been acquainted with this key, believing that it connects us to other dimensions. To discover the golden mean in some ancient building is like getting greetings from the past, from the architect/builder who, by making use of this traditional knowledge, both preserved it and handed it down.

In the pleasant daylight not long after sunrise, I cannot distinguish the infinitude of stars in the skies. According to my senses, it is a dome of blue that arches protectively over the reality of my existence as in a crystal globe in which snowflakes lie quiescent before somebody shakes it. So my perception of a bright, empty space that gifts me with early morning tranquility runs counter to my mental awareness of the existence of vibrations, frequencies and waves abounding in outer space.

Returning home, I negotiate the countless steps up the gravel hillside. Splendid hotels and apartment houses have positioned themselves along the front line facing the sea. Holiday makers frequent Netanya in droves every summer, the French having a particular affection for the place. This is the Israeli Riviera—a multicultural meeting point for the traditions of the Middle East and Europe with a touch of North Africa and a generous helping of the culture of our immigrants from the former Soviet Union. I pass them on their morning strolls along the promenade, or limbering up, using various kinds of outdoor fitness equipment. It is through their eyes that we have learned once more to appreciate beach, sea and sun.

Man and Nature—the story of a long relationship. At first, everything seemed perfect—a veritable paradise. Watching nature channels on TV, I marvel at any untamed, virginal landscape, at any ancient splendor, its serenity undisturbed by human intervention. So the Creator, viewing His work, must have marveled and seen that it was good.

That bite out of the apple from the Tree of Knowledge of Good and of Evil most probably made us more critical. Suddenly, the Garden of Eden was no longer such a paradise! What a fall! Discovering shortcomings, Man started to complain: it was too cold for him, it was too hot; his food lacked variety… he decided to change his surroundings: "If this mountain is in our way, we will flatten it…. "If the plain is monotonous or boring, we will construct hanging gardens for our delight…. "We need a bridge to get to the opposite bank of the river…. We must discover what is over there, beyond the great sea."

This urge to intervene and change things may well derive from man's survival software, a state of awareness that evolved as man separated himself from Nature, even coming to regard Nature as hostile to his own existence. There emerged an individual who acts upon Nature, who uses tools and technology. A part of his deep inner promptings consist of the motivation to change things or, as he experiences it, to improve them.

Yet, some of Earth's civilizations still preserve the concept of Paradise, which holds that the world, as created, is perfect. It can be found, for example, in the tradition of the Aborigines of Australia. Their historic memory stretches back thousands of years, long before the advent of the white man. Fortunately for us, the chain remained unbroken, and we can hear their message as it emanates over time. Their version of how men came into being is that humans received Earth from the creating ancestors in order to preserve it in its pristine state as it was on the first day of Creation; and theirs is a clear and detailed tradition of how to be partners in the day-to-day maintenance of Paradise on both the physical and on the energetic levels. The Garden of Eden was given to them in a state of perfection as a living body with coordinated parts and pulsating with a regular beat—a dream that comes true.

Back home, I start hunting for an idea I came across in a book by Steven McFadden, (*Ancient Voices Current Affairs*) in which he cites remarks by the an aboriginal wise woman called Alinta (Lorraine Mafi Williams). I wanted to include the aborigines in my story, because they are one of the most ancient sources indicative of our originating from elsewhere in the universe. For now, this message will serve us as a reminder, like a refrigerator sticker: "We originate from the stars."

TIME TO TELL EVERYONE

We, the Australian Aboriginals, have been on our traditional land, the Land of the Everlasting Spirit, for tens of thousands of years. Our culture is rivaled by no other, though we have been in seclusion for the last two hundred years. We are re-emerging from that seclusion now to show ourselves as no one has ever seen us. Our creation stories take us back into the Dreamtime, beginning when the Earth was one land mass. At that time the four races—red, yellow, black, and white—lived side by side. There, they lived as one people, creating a world of harmony, balance and mystery.

As Aboriginals we have kept our culture intact for thousands of years into the present time. Now we are ready to share our wondrous culture with the other people of the world. That is my work through my teaching and my films.

What a lot of people tend to forget is that my country has only been occupied for two hundred years by the British. It took the white people only fifty years to destroy a million years of our culture, but the core of it still remains strong. We haven't forgotten. Our elders are telling us to go out and tell everyone, so that no one can say they didn't hear.

LAND OF THE EVERLASTING SPIRIT

Whenever our elders or shaman people—all our elders are shaman people—talk about our history and our beginning, our creation, they always talk about the time when the Earth was one land mass. They speak of time before the cataclysm came that split the Earth up into the continents.

This is our story, our mythology. Our land, Australia is called Arunta, the Land of the Everlasting Spirit. Our old people tell us that we originally came from a planet that had seen its time and just blew up.

See, our people were like refugees, and they went and lived in the stars in the Milky Way. Then seven spirit brothers and seven spirit sisters came to Earth. They came when the Earth was one big land mass.

They came to erect an energy grid. Because, you see, the planet Earth is among the smallest of planets. And it is really not in the galactic system where all the other planets exist. We believe Earth is just a little bit outside the plane of the Milky Way galaxy in space. Because the Earth is so small, when the planets line up in a certain way the pull of the galactic energy is so strong that it could just suck planet Earth into the spiral plane of the galactic system and toss it all around.

So, my people were given the knowledge to create this energy grid because the planet that they were previously on did not have such a protective structure, and it was destroyed. They realized that their new home, Earth, needed to have such an energy grid in a strong, healthy condition to withstand periodic energy pulsations from the galaxy.

Otherwise, it would quickly be drawn into the plane of the galaxy and experience devastating turbulence.

But my ancestors had learned this lesson, and so they came to Earth to erect an energy grid, or an Earth truss, to help the Earth when it undergoes its changes. My ancestors' responsibility and my people's responsibility still are to the energy grid.

The protective structure that Lorraine refers to is the system of energy lines (ley lines) that runs into the interior of the planet and all around it. As a system, it resembles the system of meridians in the human body that is used in acupuncture treatment.

THE SACRED RAINBOW SERPENT

In our old way we call the energy grid Boamie, the Sacred Rainbow Serpent, whose colors reflect the beauty of the Earth and sky, the Rainbow. The multicolored coils of the Rainbow Serpent are reflected in the precious stones that are concealed in the Earth's crust. It is called the Rainbow Serpent because it has all the colors of the rainbow, gold and silver, of course, and the diamonds, the rubies, the emeralds, and the uranium. You see, it is the foundation, the Earth's crust. They are the particular substances that keep the energy grid strong and the Earth solid when the planets line up every so often and threaten to draw the Earth into the galactic energy swirl.

Since my people erected the energy grid, the Earth just sort of sails through the periodic planetary lineups without any difficulties. So that's my people's responsibility. Both men and women are very knowledgeable in how the energy grid works for the whole system. We know what each mineral in the Earth is supposed to do, and what men's and women's responsibilities are to keep the grid strong and healthy.

THE BALANCE IS IN JEOPARDY

We are very concerned about the energy grids of the Earth. They are there to help the Earth maintain its balance. Crystals and other minerals feed energy to the energy grid. They have been used for millions of years that way. For the health of the Earth, the crystals must be free to let energy flow to the grid.

But now minerals, metals and jewels have been removed from the Earth to such an extent that the balance is in jeopardy. Uranium, in particular, is important for this task. When it is all gone, the Earth will be right out of balance.

This mining has an influence on the human race, too, and the human body. The human being is a link between the Heavens and the Earth. By keeping our bodies in balance and harmony, we can keep the Earth healthy, and that in turn supports our health. You see, it's a cycle. I use crystals in healing, but I do not believe they should be taken from the Earth to be used as ornaments. It's more valuable to leave them in the Earth. The same applies with uranium.

AT A CRUCIAL JUNCTURE

The tradition from which Lorraine comes, and the meetings held during this time by the wise men of the tribe, speak of the fact that we have reached a turning point, a crucial junction in human history.

We have been told that within every one million years, there is a seven-thousand-year-long Earth shift. Then we begin to go into a new world, like we are doing now. By our reckoning, we are actually at the end of a seven-thousand-year shift now and we are beginning to enter a new million-year-long epoch.

Our people and our teachings are very similar to the teachings of the North American Indians. But we have different interpretations and we know our responsibility—taking care of the Earth through the energy grids. We perform our task by giving thanks to the Earth through the songs, dances and ceremonies.

Right now there are two things. The Earth is undergoing its earthly changes, which is normal for this time in our development. But because there's been so much destruction to the energy grid, especially the gold, which is nearly exhausted already—and now they are after the uranium—there is great danger to the stability of the Earth.

Gold has driven men mad for thousands of years, leading them to lie, steal, cheat, murder, and make war…all this wickedness to get the gold. Humanity has become greedy and as a result, wicked. That has led to fighting, war, and disease. People have forgotten their responsibility to the Earth, for want of the gold. And now it's the uranium.

As well as the Earth, humanity has to go though its changes. We've all got to rejuvenate and to create a new world on this same physical substance. And we are going through it. There's no safe place on Earth. We've just got to ride it out, but if we are in balance within ourselves and in balance with the Earth, then we are healthy.

At the end of each change—every time we come into a new world—the Great Creator says: 'OK humanity, you must start your change now, too, and go into the new world—but you must do it in accordance with the Earth, as well as yourself, with heart.'

What has become apparent within the last decades is the enormous scope of the task of repairing the damage that humanity has inflicted on the planet during the technological age. Many men and women worldwide have heard the call to do whatever lies within their power to avert the total destruction of the Earth and to create good living conditions for future generations. I believe, like so many others, that I too have been summoned to render assistance in this important task of repairing the energy grid that enfolds the planet, while activating and intensifying the energy at focal hubs and linking them together. Other people have been given different segments of the grid. Over time I have learned that other geobiologists have received messages similar to the one I received. The mystic knowledge that lies hidden in each individual's heart concerning the important task he is due to fulfill in the service of Mother Earth translates itself into hands-on practice. Geobiologists are using know-how that has been handed down from one generation to the next, gaining sophistication along the way, so as to be able to help humanity survive and evolve to the next phase.

1... About Geobiology

Geobiology is best explained as an applied field designed to create energetic harmony in the relationship between people and the neighborhood in which they live. The word "geobiology" derives from "geo" —meaning Earth and from "bio" —life, and it is a science that engages in the research of the influence of the Earth on man and on all other living creatures. This is an ancient field of learning, its mysterious origins lost somewhere far back in the mists of time. Much evidence of its use has been found as far back as 13,500 BCE, in Africa, in North America and in the temples of ancient Egypt and, indeed, throughout Mesopotamia. On the Golan Heights, for example, uncut basaltic field stones, arranged in multiple concentric circles surrounding a central cairn were found in 1967. This location, Rujm-el-Hiri (Stone Heap of the Wild Cat), dates back more than 4500 years and was a megalithic complex used for rituals. Dolmens throughout Europe and even in Israel (in Gamla) are another attestation of the use and knowledge of form and energy.

The energetic properties of a particular location were taken into consideration when erecting a building for religious ritual, such that the edifice will contribute to the spiritual development of its congregation. This practice has been actively preserved in Europe due in part, to the ongoing existence of societies and orders (the Free Masons or the Knights Templar, for example) and also of builders' guilds in times when the great churches and cathedrals were being erected. Likewise, the "water finders" who preserved and handed down techniques known as "dowsing" or "radiesthesia" that currently form part of the practice of geobiology, have all contributed to the preservation and handing down of a most valuable tradition. Fortunately this know-how is currently enjoying a revival and is presently evolving in line with contemporary scientific methods.

Ideally, housing should be constructed in such a way as to take environmental conditions into consideration. We know that in the past, people resorted to the services of dowsers, who were the forerunners of today's geobiologists, before commencing any building work. The dowsers operated by means of divining rods or a pendulum. The dowsers would test for the presence of subterranean currents of water or faults. These singularities exert a negative influence on the health of the humans dwelling above, over lengthy periods of time. For many years, people preserved the know-how of how to build in such a way as to raise the vitality of people visiting synagogues, churches and other public edifices. Research that I conducted into cathedrals, churches and monasteries indicates that the role of the dowser was vital in the planning of the construction, the precise location, the inner proportions, and the various ornaments. The dowser's identity, however, remained secret, as a member of a builder's guild. The spiritual message was conveyed in stone, but few today are able to read the language in which it was written.

Present day construction gives no heed to the subterranean properties of the land, nor does it boost positive energies as it could and should. The result of improper construction is cumulative damage that finds expression in the diseases that attack the householders. The disturbances that are to be found in one's dwelling place are called geopathic phenomena and fall into a number of categories:

> Subterranean water currents—these naturally exist everywhere, but when flowing beneath a building they cause arthritis, degenerative rheumatism, sleeplessness, chronic fatigue, and so forth.

Subterranean faults and cavities—these are especially harmful if they are located beneath a bed, a work station, or wherever people spend a great deal of time. Health damage can manifest as cancer.

Telluric grids—these are electromagnetic-radiation networks that cover the Earth's mantle. One of the most well-known networks, the Hartmann network, has regularly disposed lines (every 2 to 2.5 meters),[1] oriented south to north and west to east. Hartmann lines are the result of nickel in the core of the planet. Another popular network is the Curry network, whose lines run at 45° to the Hartmann network. These are irregularly spaced (anywhere from 2 to 13 meters)[2] and are derived from the iron in the Earth's nucleus. I consider and teach that all these lines are harmful, and their effect is felt most strongly at points where they interconnect. A crossing of a Curry-line network, when combined with a water current beneath a bed, is liable, over time, to cause cancer or a heart attack. Originally, at Creation, the lines had no harmful effect on humans, but as people began polluting and created violence, the lines turned negative.

Cosmo-Telluric chimneys—simply put, these are invisible, living entities whose function is to purify the astral/energetic envelope of the planet. They travel freely over the telluric grids and stop at certain advantageous locations. Since these entities are attracted by energy, there are beneficial chimneys in high-energy locations and usually there are harmful ones in homes that have low-level energies due to underground currents.

EVERYTHING VIBRATES

Life energy is all pervasive. It is what the Chinese call Chi, and as it is well known, I will not give a review here of all the definitions of energy in the course of history, from the time of Paracelsus to that of Wilhelm Reich.

We now know, for example, that thought energy is transmitted via electrical signals in the brain that create a field that spreads in ripples in a manner resembling the operation of a radio transmitter. We are affected by the vibrations of various force fields that are transmitted to us by others, and we too, in our turn, influence our surroundings in like manner. In effect, our body

---

1. 6.5 to 8 ft.
2. 6.5 to 42.7 ft.

tries to adapt and adjust itself to the conditions of its environment. The cells in our body have a frequency of their own; and the environment transmits a frequency that is different from the base frequency of the cell. The cell endeavors to revert to its own base frequency, and these efforts cause it to lose strength to the point where it ceases to function on its own frequency, i.e. it surrenders to the frequency of its surroundings. The environmental frequency starts to alter the internal structure of the cell.

The energetic level of a location defines the life quality of the people living there. If the level is reasonable or high, those who live in the house will enjoy peace of mind and good health. If the energetic level is low, they will live lives of tension, expressed in friction within the family. Over the years, the low energy will cause health problems.

How fit a place is for human habitation can be measured by examining the following variables—vital-energy level, the level of the Earth's natural magnetic field, and the frequency/color of the energy. These data can be obtained with the aid of radiesthesia[1] tools.

The vital-energy level of any site may be measured in Bovis units, so called after Antoine Bovis (1871–1947), a scientist who made a very substantial contribution to the field of radiesthesia. The Bovis scale gives an indication of the vitality of a location, object, food or a person's state of health.

The measurement system of radiesthesia is composed of the individual taking the measurement, the pendulum and the Bovis scale. Measurements are therefore dependent on the person taking them and on his physical, energetic, spiritual and mental condition. This concept is difficult for conventional science to accept, since we are accustomed to physical measuring instruments operating, as it were, objectively, unaffected by the researcher; yet quantum physics has proved to us that it is not really possible to separate the researcher from the object of his investigation—that the observer greatly influences the results. If so, then despite the relativity of the measurement and the possibility that different individuals will arrive at a different measurement, the work of the geobiologist and his investigations are guided by this measurement method. My own experience suggests that a "constant" emerges in my measurements, providing high precision in my results.

Various problems in the situation of buildings are revealed by means of dowsing rods (or antennas) and a pendulum; these tools facilitate the diagnosis for determining the energetic level of a house or public building in accordance

---

1. Radiesthesia is the ability to detect subtle radiation within the human body. All human bodies give off unique or characteristic emissions, as do all other physical bodies or objects. Such a radiation field is often termed an aura.

with clearly defined parameters. Most cases call for the intervention of the geobiologist. In professional jargon this is referred to as "harmonization" —the creation of a balance of frequencies that is carried out with the aid of the geobiologist's highly developed capability for energetic sensing and in cooperation with the intelligence of Nature.

DEFINING POSITIVE AND NEGATIVE

Throughout this book, negative and positive are used. These terms are commonly applied to power cells having positive and negative terminals. In Geobiology, these terms can be used to mean a number of things. When using a dowsing pendulum, there is a convention applied: The rotation can be clockwise (CW), defined as positive, or the rotation can be counter-clockwise (CCW), defined as negative.

These terms can be used to express the influence of some parameter on our well-being: Positive implies that the influence is beneficial (such as being in a cathedral); negative means that the influence has a deleterious effect on our health (such as an underground fault).

THE MAGNETIC FIELDS

We are always within the magnetic field of the terrestrial globe. The existence of this field is vital for every living organism. Accordingly, prolonged presence in a location where the magnetic field is not optimal causes gradual injury to our health. What reduces the level of the natural magnetic field? There are several possible causes: a large accumulation of metal, subterranean water currents, subterranean faults or cavities (natural grottoes, underground caves or subway tunnels). Once the negative effect of the water currents are neutralized and blocked by means of mental intervention, the magnetic field rises.

Matter is in a state of constant internal flux and in molecular interaction with its surroundings. It transmits and receives waves of energy on various frequencies. An energy frequency that is created expresses itself as a wavelength and also appears on the color spectrum. Frequencies may be visible or invisible to the human eye.

The French researcher Belizal discovered a correlation between the color spectrum and electromagnetic waves. (See illustration on 24.) Radiesthesia adopted Belizal's spectrum and uses it as a work graph. It is a circle that is divided into two sectors: one electrical and one magnetic. Belizal demonstrated that the colors in the magnetic phase are beneficial to man, whereas the colors in the electrical phase are harmful to him. The following are some examples of phases/colors:

The white frequency appears on the graph in the magnetic phase, and is found in a spiritual location with very high energy (such as cathedrals).

The violet frequency, in the magnetic phase, vibrates on a very high positive level, which is beneficial to man. We frequently find it in houses after harmonization work has been carried out.

The orange frequency, in the negative, electric phase, is frequently found in a home prior to energetic cleansing and shows that geopathic problems exist there.

The red frequency appears on the graph in the electrical-phase sector and is found in places where there is or has been a great deal of suffering or spilling of blood, or where the location has been destroyed by fire.

The green frequency, as an invisible color, appearing on Belizal's graph in the electrical phase, is negative and is found at locations where people and animals have been tortured or offered as sacrifices.

The black frequency appears on the graph in the electrical phase; it is very negative and represents death or a place where people have been buried.

Although several methods and means are employed by other geobiologists, I do my work by means of mental intervention. Mental intervention uses thought energy which it channels to a specific object or place. I know how to focus my intent in order to implement a diverse range of actions such as blocking subterranean water currents, diverting energy lines, relocating energy chimneys from one place to another; and I am assisted in this by the forces of Nature. My purpose is to cleanse the house of problems that cause the tenants' distress and poor health. The process of harmonization is aimed at the creation of harmony among various elements found in Nature and between man and his environment.

I have frequently had the opportunity to measure apartments and houses whose locations were extremely negative, with an energy level of 4,000 Bovis or less. These were houses that were located over subterranean currents or faults. Following harmonization, the energy level of the house can reach as high as 60,000 Bovis, an energy level that facilitates well being and good health. This positive level attracts more and more vitality, which we experience as joy.

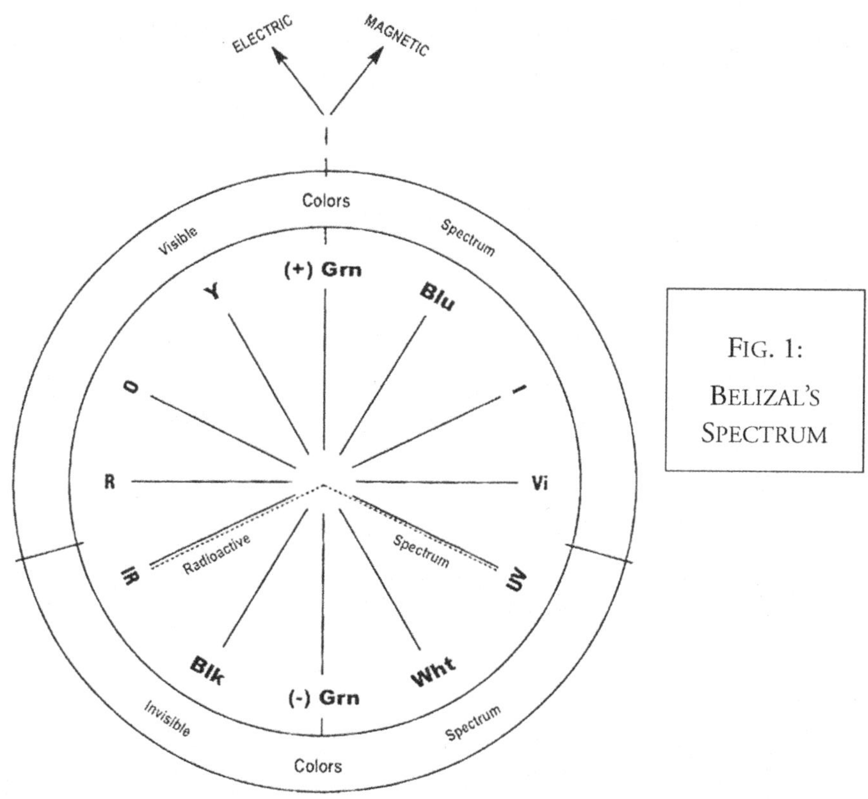

FIG. 1:

BELIZAL'S SPECTRUM

The geobiologist's vision also extends to the current state of Mother Earth. According to measurements taken in the 20th century, the average rate of the energy level of the terrestrial globe was estimated at about 6,500 Bovis. Over a period of years it jumped to 10,000 Bovis. The current level is estimated at about 14,000 Bovis, and that level continues to rise. This is the energy level in a neutral location that neither scatters energy nor steals it from those present.

2... My Early Life

On November 8, 1942, Allied troops landed in Algeria, arriving two days ahead of the German army that was about to invade the country, attacking primarily the port town of Mers-El-Kébir. My life commenced shortly thereafter, on June 15, 1943, in the town of Oran, in my grandmother's bed. It was a difficult beginning. Just as my mother was going into labor, German planes started bombing the town where we lived. I was in no hurry to come out. Perhaps, I was aware of what awaited me out there, as forceps had to be used to facilitate my debut into this world.

Once the war was over, life returned to normal. Being the first son, I had the whole household dancing attendance on me. In fact, until the age of ten, I grew up as an only child, because it wasn't until then that my younger brother, Jean-Yves was born. Rumor has it that I was a good-tempered, likeable child, showing curiosity about everything mechanical or technical. I demonstrated great patience in dismantling and reassembling mechanical and electrical appliances, but I also liked sewing clothes for dolls and doing anything, in fact, that called for precision and an investment of time.

I was raised in the spirit of French culture. My family, although completely secular, did observe a number of traditional customs, celebrating holy days and festivals in token of its belonging to the Jewish community of Algeria. Almost every Jew born in North Africa currently boasts a grandpa who was, in his day, a Kabbalist rabbi, widely famed and influential among his community. When I began to take an interest in the spiritual domain, I, too, sought some spiritual affinity being bequeathed through my family; and sure enough, I found that my maternal great-grandfather, Rabbi David Chouraki, had possessed extensive knowledge of Torah and Kabbala and was known for having foretold things that were about to happen. He had been, my mother said, a holy man; and after he died, his family continued to pray to him in times of trouble, seeking to use his merit and have him intercede on their behalf, from above.

In 1956, as the winds of Algeria's War of Independence started to blow, the security of that country's Jewish population became undermined. My parents decided to emigrate to the United States. At the age of 13, I discovered a new world and a new language, its melody totally different from the lilt of my mother tongue—French. In high school I was dubbed "Frenchy," but that didn't stop me from becoming popular, a fairly good student and a Boy Scout.

In retrospect, it seems that the traits I had acquired in childhood are proving useful to my professional life as an adult. These qualities reinforced my technical inclinations, causing me to choose an engineering career, and subsequently proved very useful to me in my profession as a geobiologist. I refer mainly to the qualities of patience, accuracy, and the ability to concentrate on a subject in a focused manner and over a long period of time.

In the snowbound winters of Philadelphia, with Paul Anka's songs playing in the background, I used my free time to build a huge model of the battleship Missouri. On board this ship, the Japanese signed their surrender in World War II. In 1959, cradling this enormous artifact in my arms, I went to visit my uncle in Algeria, and I had to come up with some convincing explanation for customs at the stopover in Paris.

After high school, I attended college for a year, but I could not settle down. Abandoning my studies, I joined the US military, where I served three years as a communications and electronics technician. After that, I started work at Philco-Ford, where I remained for ten years. My job enabled me to see the world, and I was sent to resolve technical problems in Japan, Vietnam, Iran, Thailand, Korea, Germany and Israel.

In 1966, after my return from Vietnam and Thailand, where I was working as a technician for Philco-Ford, I met a lovely girl, Florence. We were married and lived happily for eight years. She was a wonderful woman. Everybody liked her. Then why leave her? I know today that I was guided to take this step, even though it had no logic and made no sense at the time.

During my fourth trip to Israel, in 1974, I met someone who was to change my life—a good looking young girl soldier named Ora. I spent an evening with her and ultimately found myself at the wheel of the rental car I had parked on the Tel Aviv beach, gazing at the sky. I looked at the moon and experienced a sensation that was at once strong and strange. I started to cry for no apparent reason. It was a decisive moment, whose true meaning and function for me I would only discover much later.

Returning to the U. S., I tried to keep up my comfortable life, and familiar routine, but a small inner voice was constantly urging me to leave everything, return to Israel and settle there. After a fairly difficult inner struggle, I reached a decision: I separated from my wife of eight years, left my excellent job and, in defiance of all logic, emigrated to Israel. At the age of 31, I had to start all over again, from zero. It was a difficult time, whichever way you looked at it. I gradually built myself a life: I married Ora, and fathered four sons.

For six years I worked at a high-tech company where I began to be considered an expert in technical writing. I was soon swamped with requests from various sources, and I decided to become self-employed. This was a challenging time, professionally speaking, and also a very busy one. While I was knee-deep in technical documents and books, Ora was engaging in reflexology, meditation, astrology and acupuncture. Being curious by nature, I began to study healing. During my first lesson, I developed a violent headache that lasted several days, which led to my decision to consult a healer named Yemima, a woman of French extraction, who later became a well-known spiritual teacher in Israel. She gave me hands-on treatment, touched my head and gesticulated while facing me. The pain went away. For me at that time, it was truly a miracle.

This was when it could be said that my mind opened up. Thanks to Ora, I began visiting personal-growth workshops, getting body-soul treatments and attending festivals. One day, at an alternative-medicine exhibition, a book at one of the stalls caught my eye—*Nothing In This Book Is True, But It's Exactly*

How Things Are. In this book, author Bob Frissel, mainly tells the story of Drunvalo Melchizedek, who through his books, especially his book on *The Ancient Secret of the Flower of Life*, taught a path to perfect health.

Shortly after that, I photocopied a page out of a Hebrew magazine that dealt with spirituality. When I went to return it to its owner, an English-language website[1] caught my eye. I took it as a sign that I should attend a seminar being conducted by Drunvalo himself, who, wonderfully enough, was about to visit Israel.

The four-day seminar addressed several topics, which would later become highly relevant to the task I was meant to undertake—one related to the healing of the planet. When Drunvalo introduced the topic of geobiology[2], a clear understanding came to me that this was my path. Old memories seemed to have stirred in me, because the subject awoke in me knowledge that I had possessed long ago since, and that had perhaps lain concealed in my brain cells awaiting an opportune moment. Even Socrates, after all, tried to prove that the entire learning process is nothing but remembering....

After the seminar, I started to delve into geobiology; and to that end, I travelled to the United States and France to study. Back in Israel, I began lecturing to spread the good tidings of geobiology.

Another message concerning the direction I must choose reached me through a spiritual workshop conducted in the Sinai desert. There, with a small group, I spent six days in the heart of the desert, isolated totally from the outside world. One night, under a starry sky, our teacher, a gifted medium, told us about a previous life each one of us had lived. I felt open and tranquil, thanks to the magical energy that pervaded the desert. When my turn came, the instructress told me that in the age of Atlantis and Lemuria (about 13,000 BCE), I was a Lemurian. I was greatly attracted by the technology of the Atlanteans, rivals of the Lemurians. The Lemurian civilization was technologically underdeveloped, but they had another secret that the Atlanteans longed to get their hands on.

In my eagerness to learn the secrets of the technology, I revealed to them the Lemurians' secret of love. Yes, love was both the source of their strength and the key to their weakness. By means of this information, the Atlanteans started using emotional manipulation in order to gain control over their enemies.

---

1. http://www.solischool.org, formerly FlowerOfLife.com
2. Geobiology is the scientific study of the Earth as a living system.

Quite unexpectedly, this story resonated powerfully with me. I was deeply moved. My technically and scientifically oriented training had never exposed me to the possibility of the existence of civilizations of this sort. That night, I lay sleepless. As dawn rose, we left the oasis, heading for the hills, where each of us would meditate in isolation. Seated on a mound in the middle of nowhere, I mused on the tale of Lemuria.

Alone with my thoughts, I realized why I was being drawn to geobiology: this is work that necessitates contact with the terrestrial globe and is intended to help heal Mother Earth. Until then, I had been unaware of my destiny, but, sitting there alone, in the middle of nowhere, I realized that I had a debt to repay: I have returned to Earth to make up for lost time. I apologized to our Mother Earth; I wept with all my heart and soul, until the sound of my weeping reached over the distance to where my friends could hear it. After a time, I sensed that I was forgiven, and this was the beginning of my new life.

The world of technology ceased to interest me. I gradually converted from engineer to geobiologist, engaging in both professions simultaneously for several years. My new assignment, that of helping people to live better, came to occupy an ever greater part of my life, ultimately becoming my sole occupation.

I dedicated myself to geobiology with enthusiasm, desiring to continue passing it on to others. So it came about that I began to teach geobiology, at first as part of Feng Shui courses given by other teachers, and later in workshops that I organized in Israel, France, Spain, the Ivory Coast, and Portugal. Projects undertaking the energetic purification of private homes brought about an improvement in the quality of life and health of the residents; in some cases, I would treat an entire neighborhood or community, and I was privileged to create harmony between people and their environment. I chalked up a great deal of experience, and there was no lack of opportunity to improve my techniques and the processes I was using.

I became curious about past building methods, and in particular, I began researching the energy parameters found in places of prayer and worship. Again and again I found proof that men erecting buildings in the past were fully aware of the existence of subterranean water currents, faults in the crust of the Earth, and the telluric lines circling the globe; these people also knew of energy-producing vortices that influence the human energy field. Over many generations, care was taken in selecting the construction sites, and the building took into account the particular conditions of each location. When erecting synagogues, churches or cathedrals, the builders harnessed those elements of the local conditions, which enabled positive energy to be generated for the benefit of whomever came to their doors.

While enjoying my new path and researching its past sources with great interest, I still could not guess what the future held for me. Had anyone told me, I would have found it hard to believe.

3... My New Family

During my first trip to Africa, to Abidjan in the Ivory Coast, I met a widely travelled Israeli businessman. He told me he had been pursuing spiritual studies for many years, and as our conversation generated an atmosphere of trust, Géèma (as I will call him in this book), told me that he has a contact with a group of entities that exist beyond the physical plane. The group calls itself "the Family."

Luckily, by the time I met Géèma, I had already encountered several ideas that made me expand my belief system to include the reality he was talking about. This was because working with Nature's intelligence involves acknowledging the existence of non-physical beings, of invisible helpers such as angels, as well as the possibility of chance encounters with the trapped souls of individuals who passed away. This understanding enabled me to accept Géèma's remarks with relative equanimity. I also realized that it was not a coincidence that we had met. Rather, this encounter was part of my path.

It seemed that my new friend and I had a lot in common. He, too, had studied geobiology and other esoteric subjects. Moreover, both of us found ourselves divorced at our advanced chronological age (while still very young at heart, of course, and fit enough physically to go skipping over the hills, as I relate below). By then, our children were all grown, so our time was at hand, meaning that we were free to do whatever needed to be done with it.

Socially, I had always had plenty of people around, most of whom were friends of my ex-wife, Ora, who was involved with the spiritual community in Israel, teaching and lecturing on topics such as natural health; and our home had always extended a warm welcome to "free spirits." But I didn't find my place there, even though several ties had been forged. When I connected with someone from a deep place, that person became like a brother to me. That is how it was with Géèma.

The conscious recognition of the existence of "the Family" became highly meaningful for me. Now I could connect all the dots of my past history into a coherent picture. My life, I realized, had been scattered with signposts pointing me in the right direction. And I understood that I was still being guided by "the Family" so that I would accomplish all the missions that had been entrusted to me in this lifetime. This understanding also involved acknowledging that my encounters with people had not happened by chance. I travel a great deal, teaching geobiology around the world. Students have become colleagues. A true alliance has sprung up between us, with work jointly undertaken for the benefit of people in the country in which they live, and beyond it, for the benefit of Mother Earth.

4... Entities of Another Kind

In our reality, there is more than meets the eye, so I urge you to understand two significant, although invisible, phenomena: chimneys (also known as cosmotelluric chimneys) and vortices. They are a part of this great organism that we call Mother Earth, and they allow this living planet to function in the same way that our body functions—it breathes, pulsates and metabolizes.

Chimneys and vortices are of priceless importance for the health of the planet. It is essential and vital that they function at full force in order to cleanse the noosphere (the energetic, mental plane) and renew the Earth's energetic envelope. The entire system is constantly acting to repair the damages caused by technology and humanity's negative energies, in an attempt to achieve balance and harmony.

As I mentioned, my task as a geobiologist is to assist this process. The rapidity with which the condition of Mother Earth has deteriorated necessitates a serious rehabilitation of the energy-regulation system. In practical terms, as I will describe in connection with my work at the 18 sites in Israel, I have activated vortices and chimneys and linked them together. When I use the term "activation," I refer to a mental intervention aimed at restarting dormant chimneys, followed by measuring their energy immediately afterwards and making sure there was a distinct increase in their vibration levels.

The fact that the parameters of a chimney can show an increase in vitality leads me to regard it as a living entity. Not exactly in the sense in which this faculty of "life" is generally attributed to humans, animals or even plants, but living nonetheless, and able to be either positive or negative.

In the course of my work of cleansing properties and houses, I have always come across negative chimneys. Mostly, they are situated in the bedroom, on the bed. I have made this discovery dozens of times. People occupying these rooms at night either have difficulty falling asleep, sleep badly, suffer from nightmares, and awake as tired as if they had been fighting throughout the night. In such cases, I transpose the chimneys outside the house. I also create a defensive wall around the house, thus preventing new chimneys from entering the premises.

In high-energy locations, I have always discovered positive chimneys. Positive places attract positive chimneys and negative places attract negative chimneys. Some of the chimneys have presumably been on Earth for tens if not hundreds of thousands of years; while others are newer. In dwellings, negative chimneys can persist or be attracted by the strong negativity of the house—due to the location and/or due to the occupants. They are usually located over the bed because they are attracted by the energy of the occupants who spend a lot of uninterrupted time there. Chimneys have no intentions of their own.

They may, however, arouse unpleasant sensations. Indeed, our energy level depends partly on our immediate surroundings. If we are in a holy place, our body senses the fact; we become filled with high vibrations; we feel good; but not so in a negative location such as a prison or a hospital.

Positive chimneys are to be found everywhere in Nature and especially in spiritual places (houses of prayer and places of worship). Some came into being naturally, and others were created by people for a particular purpose.

Consider, for example, holy-water stones in churches. I have found small but highly energetic chimneys positioned in such places. A "negative" or "positive" connotation, I would like to explain, relates to the effect that the chimneys have on people's health. It happens that in Nature certain things are not always for the well being of humanity.

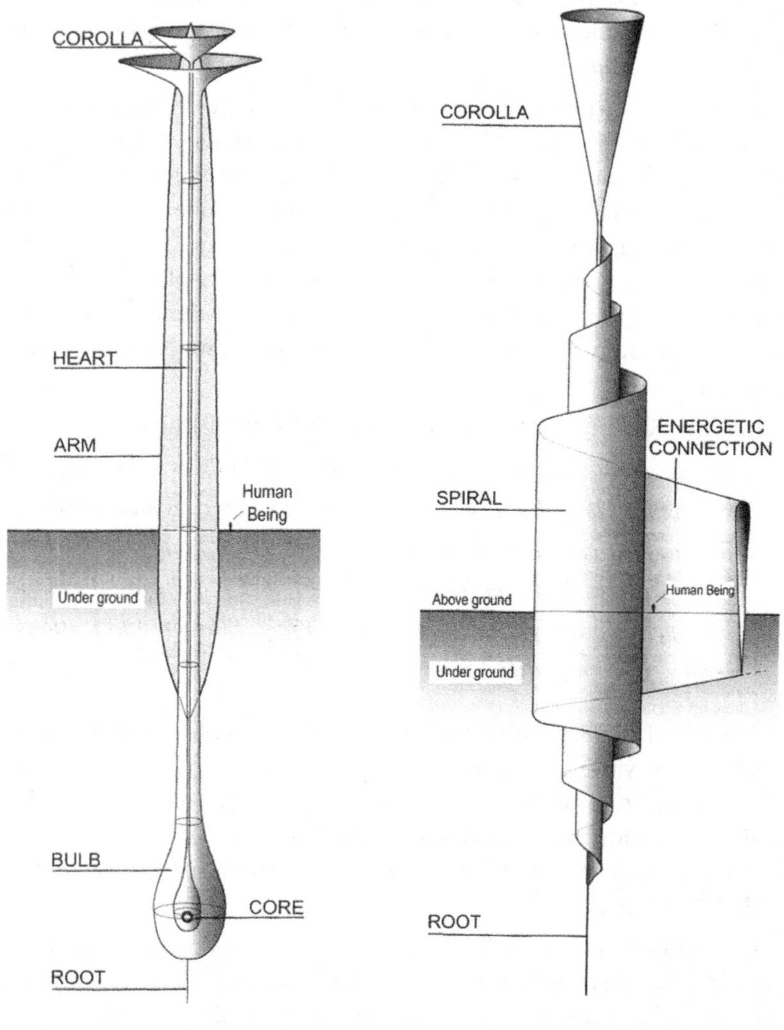

FIG 2: CHIMNEY   FIG 3: VORTEX

Even though I identify chimneys by means of tools such as a pendulum or dowsing rods, these entities can also be detected with bare hands. When the palms of your hand approaches the edge of the chimney, you may experience a tingling sensation or heat.

I have had the opportunity to measure chimneys with a diameter measuring from just a few inches to over thirty yards! Some people report chimneys with "arms," some sort of appendage hanging from them. Finding that it made no difference to the energy level of the chimney, I make no comment on these arms in my work. Apart from the diameter, the chimneys have both height and depth, and are not necessarily round. Frequently, they take an elliptic shape.

Through my study and research on chimneys, I arrived at certain insights concerning their function. The object of their existence, it seems, is to cleanse the Earth's polluted envelope. The negative energy originating in feelings and thoughts accumulates on the astral plane, becoming increasingly contaminated with what human consciousness generates. Just as people have destroyed and continue to destroy their environment on the physical plane, so do people proceed to spoil the mental plane. I also learned that the chimneys possess a collective awareness that enables them to communicate amongst themselves and with humans.

Recently Géèma received this channel from the Family:

Vortices allow extraterrestrials (ETs) from all galaxies to be teleported, to meet and to go back in the good direction. Vortices and chimneys are energetic canals, tied into different planets to supply the Earth with what she needs, for herself and for all that is living on the planet. They perform other functions, such as to facilitate communications among different entities from various galaxies."

It was as a result of "mishaps" that many discoveries came to light concerning the various properties of the chimneys. These experiences may have pulled the rug from under my feet, causing my intuition to call a halt and examine the various phenomena. I do not believe these were coincidences. I have frequently sensed that I am supposed to learn a specific lesson from these so-called "mishaps."

For example, on a certain occasion in France, I was with a group of particularly sensitive students, one of whom was indeed clairvoyant. As part of the Detailed Geobiology course, we were learning about vortices and chimneys. On the night prior to the studies, I was eating with a student at the restaurant of our place of study. I started to feel ill—so much so that I had to leave. The next day, I returned to the same spot with my class to find out what had made me feel so bad. I discovered that there was a negative chimney on the chair I had used that night. This was a great opportunity for practicing the transposition of chimneys with the students; and together, we moved the chimney outside the restaurant.

Then we drew up a list of variables related to chimneys:

Perception: The chimney could be felt, and some of us could see it. With the aid of dowsing rods, we could determine its boundaries and center. Using a pendulum, we measured the ascent/descent and rest intervals. (The ascent and descent times are defined below.)

Communication: One can communicate with a chimney. Even when activating a positive chimney, I do so by means of mental communication, as a result of which the chimney awakens and increases in size.

Cooperation: The chimney cooperates and moves according to specific requests.

Measurements: We measure the height, depth, diameter and vitality (in Bovis units) of each chimney. After activating a positive chimney, we re-measure, with the aid of a pendulum and a graph, and thus obtain an indication that the values have doubled and sometimes more than doubled.

Influence of the location: A negative chimney can make the room it is in so negative that nobody can sleep there. In addition, a negative chimney can lower the natural magnetic field where it is positioned. A positive chimney in a high-energy place, on the other hand, will bring a sense of well being and even euphoria.

Sensitivity: People have various degrees of sensitivity to chimneys. Let's take the restaurant for example. One of the students, a clairvoyant, communicated with the chimney while we were transposing it outside. Once the chimney was outside, he told us that he now had a lighter, less "rough" feeling. He stated that the chimney had expressed warmth towards him.

Motion: Experience has taught me a great deal about the modus operandi of chimneys. The root of the chimney absorbs the negative energy of the Earth and radiates it out to space. The energy discharge can last between tens of seconds and several minutes. This is the ascent time. Then there is a rest interval, a pause. After that, cosmic energy flows down and is captured by the corolla (shaped like an upside-down umbrella) of the chimney and led in the direction of the Earth. The descent time approximates the ascent time.

Formation: During my visits to Alma and Nir David (two of the 18 high-energy sites in Israel) I discovered a recurrent phenomenon: one frequently finds chimneys arranged in a triangular formation, with an energy flux circulating among them.

While doing the energetic cleansing of a hotel under construction in the Ivory Coast, I found many chimneys, some of them concentrated at the center of the hotel. There I found a large chimney, 6.4 meters[1] in diameter, and two small ones, 1.6 meters[2] in diameter, positioned alongside one another at a distance of one meter[3] from the large chimney, creating a perfect symmetry. With a sudden flash of insight I asked the pendulum whether these were a mother and two children. The answer was affirmative. This was a real discovery for me. After that, I asked Géèma to inquire with his "Family" whether this was possible.

Chimneys occur by the millions on this planet. Most have been created by Mother Earth herself. As we have mentioned, some—very few and countable—are located in churches, cathedrals, synagogues and other ancient places of worship. These were implanted by the ancient human builders. However, several chimneys were created by ETs for a number of reasons. For example, the house in Caesarea (Refer to "13... Géèma's Home" on page 77) had three such entities. Another interesting discovery is that chimneys have gender—there are masculine and feminine ones, although I found very few males. Finally, chimneys play a very important role in the purification of the planet: They pull positive energy from a gold energy ring around the planet and send the extracted negative energy from the planet to a silver ring. The process involved with these rings is described in the last chapter, "23... The Sky is Not the Limit." on page 127.

Analogy to a Radio Transceiver

While teaching a class in the Ivory Coast, I was routinely covering the subject of chimneys, when, out of the clear blue sky, my usual explanation took a turn, and I started to explain the operation of a chimney as compared to a radio transceiver (receiver/transmitter). It was clear to me that I was being fed information.

One of the basic functions of a chimney (and vortex) is to clean the Earth of negativity. This it does by absorbing the negativity via its root, during the ascending phase of its operation. The root acts as an antenna, transferring the energy to and from the chimney. The negative energy then flows into the core—in the bulb—which is like the electronic section of a transceiver. The "signals" from the Earth are transmuted to a frequency and a format that can be accepted by the cosmos. They are pulsed (just as radar signals are) so as to

---

1. 21 ft.
2. 5 ft. 3 in.
3. 3 ft. 4 in.

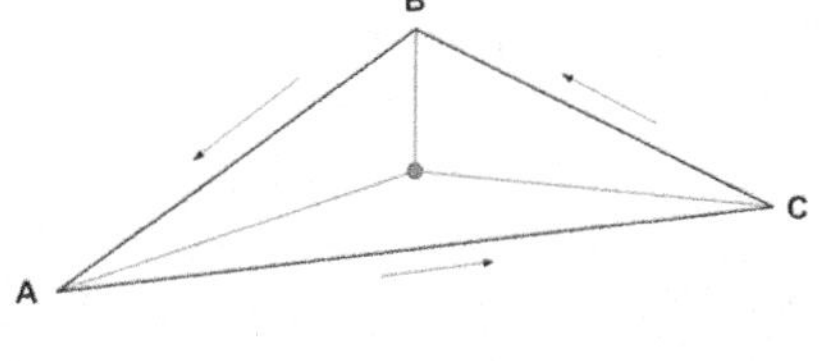

Step 1 : The three chimneys operate with rising energy (↑) ; they communicate among themselves in a circle; no communication with the center.

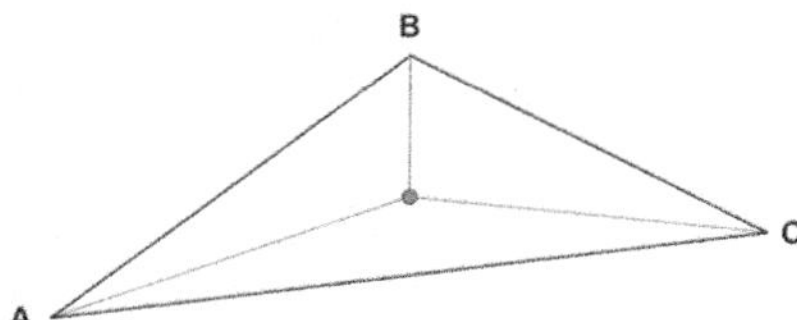

Step 2 : The three chimneys are at rest; no communication with the center.

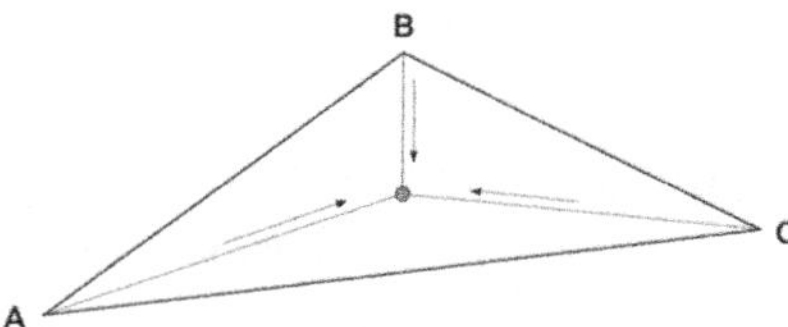

Step 3 : There is a flow of energy towards the center, from each of the three chimneys.

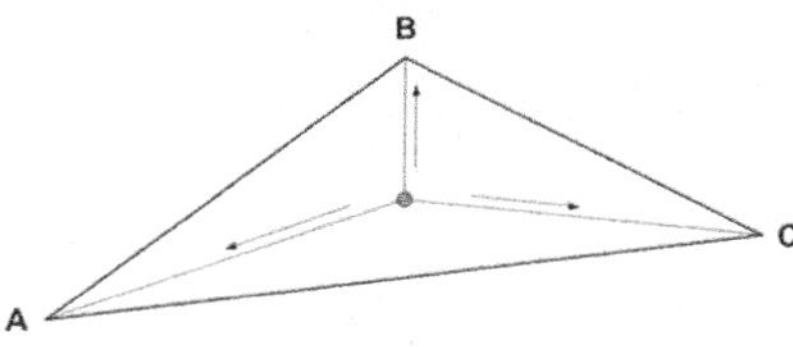

Step 4 : After a while, a flux of energy flows from the center toward the three chimneys.

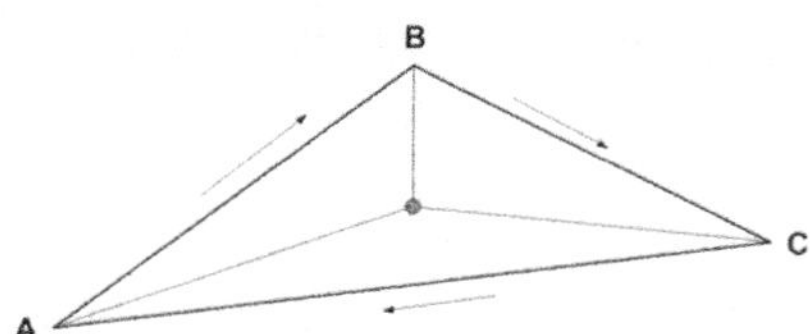

Step 5 : The three chimneys operate in falling energy (↓) ; the three chimneys communicate among themselves in a circle; no communication with the center.

FIG. 4: CHIMNEY OPERATION

insure that they will reach a long distance, out from the Earth's atmosphere. The transmission is accomplished via the small dish antenna at the very top of the chimney. The dimension of this dish causes the frequency of the transmitted signals to match that of the atmosphere. Then comes the rest period, during which a switch seems to be thrown, transferring the operation from transmission to reception. Positive energy from the cosmos is received via the larger dish whose dimension allows only positive energy to pass into the chimney. Again, the "electronic" section in the core of the bulb adapts this positive energy to the format that the Earth can best accept. The antenna or root acts as an emitting antenna to disperse the positive energy into the Earth.

ACTIVITY OF THE CHIMNEYS

In *Sacred Geometries*, Stéphane Cardinaux gives the illustrations (refer to page 19) showing the shape of the chimneys: I noticed that chimneys were constantly multiplying, making me think that Planet Earth is experiencing an ever greater need for self-cleansing.

I was asked why it is that we find both positive and negative chimneys. I suppose this is how the natural equilibrium is maintained, by means of plus and minus polarity. Chimneys are in constant motion, stopping sometimes. One thing I am sure of—negative chimneys are drawn to places where people live, to hubs of negative thoughts and feelings, and in most cases they find themselves a place in the bedroom where their presence causes health damage over time.

Vortices are spirals interconnected by an energetic link. When checked with a pendulum, they both move in a clockwise direction, then counter-clockwise, but in opposite fashion. We find vortices in Nature, but also, as I mentioned, in cathedrals and churches, usually implanted by the builders.

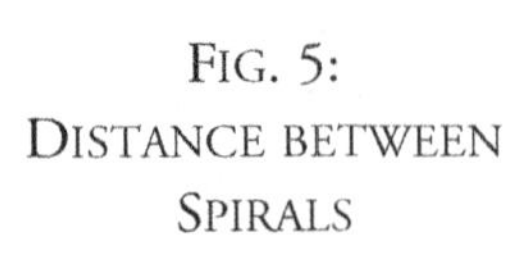

FIG. 5:
DISTANCE BETWEEN
SPIRALS

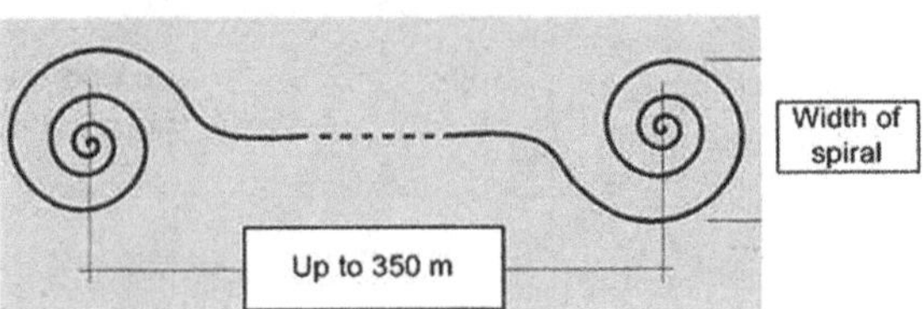

A pendulum test will show the presence of a positive spiral (moving in a clockwise direction) and a negative spiral (moving counterclockwise). (Refer to "Defining Positive and Negative" on page 5.) Their activity resembles that of a chimney, except for one difference: In a vortex, the energy of one spiral descends, while that of the other ascends. The spirals are connected by an energy link between tens of centimeters and two meters wide.[1] The width of the link is relative to the size of the spirals. The spirals of the vortex are shaped in accordance with the sixth musical note *LA*, whose frequency forms a ratio of 5/3, or 1.666. This means that the diameter of the spiral decreases according to 1.666 as one approaches the center.

I discovered a number of large spirals with a link up to 350 meters.[2] (Refer to "Fig. 5: Distance between Spirals" on page 24.) I have also seen links just a few centimeters long.[3] Those that were intentionally created by people are found in places of worship. The positive spiral will be found within the holy edifice (usually at the altar), while the negative spiral will be found outside it, in an open area. Vortex spirals can be up to 31 meters[4] in diameter. I found such spirals in a private home in Israel and will elaborate hereafter.

The object and function of vortices is to generate energy at far higher levels than those of the chimneys. People have implanted vortices, in order to raise the energy level in various locations, including places of worship, synagogues and cathedrals. Vortices are found in Nature and at pre-historic sites, evidencing the fact that ancient civilizations possessed know-how concerning them. In most of the churches I enter today, I find the same phenomenon: the positive spiral is usually at the altar, while the negative spiral is located outside the building, both spirals being connected by a link.

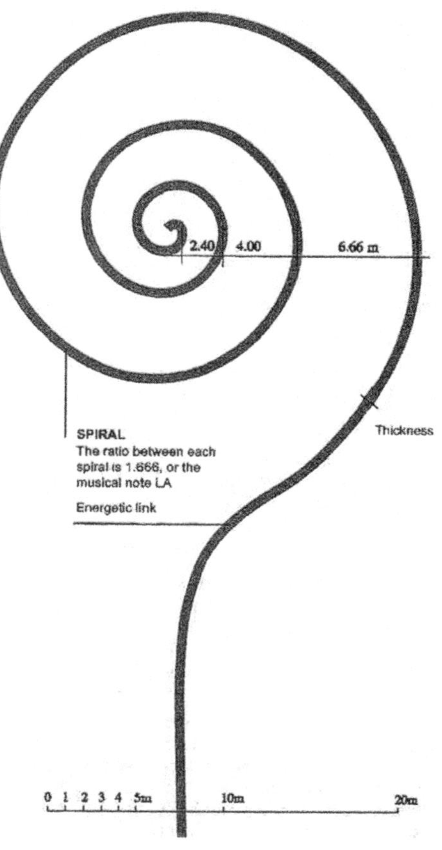

FIG. 6: FORM OF A SPIRAL

---

1. 4 in. to 6 ft. 6 in.
2. 383 yds., longer than a football field.
3. An inch or so.
4. 102 ft.

According to channeled information, both chimneys and vortices are linked to the magnetic field of Earth. The Earth is enveloped by a closely woven crisscross web, similar to a woven blanket with a mesh. The web is what keeps the magnetic field in place. Activation of chimneys and vortices helps to restore the envelope to equilibrium and wholeness.

5... The Ancient Builders

It was not by chance that those who initiated colossal building projects were rulers and kings, individuals who believed that the power over their people had been divinely delegated to them. They alone considered themselves worthy of building on a holy site—a structure that would serve as a link between Heaven and Earth. Such, of course, were the pharaohs; but this phenomenon persisted for hundreds of years, until the "modern" era, when building committees came under the responsibility of the state, and public structures were budgeted by citizens' taxes.

Over thousands of years, people lived as nomads. Even when they settled, the concept of a private home was in conformance with simple living conditions. In Mesopotamia, for example, tents were suitable for providing shelter because the weather was temperate most of the year. People also built houses with bricks of straw and clay, which were simple enough to be easily abandoned if they had to move on in search of more fertile pastures. By contrast, temples, palaces and public edifices, which were meant to stand forever, were built in accordance with clear instructions from knowledgeable individuals who had undergone an apprenticeship in the secrets of sacred geometry. They would frequently be treated as divine servants.

Contemporary geobiologists—like me—clearly identify traces of the design of those "savants" of the past. They see why a particular site was chosen, and they read the map that indicates the underlying intent of the placement of each wall—the displays, the internal proportions, the symbolic messages and the use of the technique of de-multiplying lines in order to create a cleansing effect on the visitor at the very threshold.

When I started teaching in France, I sought the best place for conducting a weekend workshop, preferably one that offered food and lodging. I had often stayed at the Reinacker Convent, near Selestat in Alsace; and it was there that my love affair with monasteries and churches began. There are some interesting churches nearby, and my students expressed the wish to hear about what I had experienced there. In the evening, after dinner, I told them of my findings concerning the occult language of church-building. At the end of the lecture, I was approached by a participant named Marie, who possesses channeling abilities; she told me that, while I was talking, she had seen me in the likeness of a master builder from the fourteenth century. This was the explanation for my being attracted to ancient churches, cathedrals and synagogues.

I struck up a friendship with a priest at the Abbatial of Neuwiller-lès-Saverne. He was a priest, but also an ardent geobiologist. I was amazed by his church and returned there several times. Together, we examined the church from the geobiological point of view and recorded our findings, which we later collated into a jointly authored book. My curiosity and interest in the energy language of churches and cathedrals continued to intensify. Later on, I was lucky enough to teach at a convent of the kind Franciscan Sisters in the township of Thal-Marmoutier, where I still teach today.

Formally, I was not very interested in stories of my past incarnations. I always tended to regard them as a waste of time, mere dramatizations of the ego. I chose rather to focus my mental energy on my work, to ensure its precision and efficiency. I sometimes think of myself as somewhat lacking in imagination, and I doubt that I could have invented the marvelous turns of events in my current incarnation, but not to worry! There are plenty of people around me who are thrilled by the magic and the adventure, who are sensitive, intuitive and attuned to the "great story." I have recourse to their ability and the messages they receive to direct my own activities.

What a marvelous bit of information it was that my student Marie brought me (there are a number of women in my life named Marie, and they are my soul sisters) concerning my being a master builder in a previous life. Could it be that today I am finding and decoding the cipher of clues that I myself buried centuries ago?

Marie gave me a handwritten page on which she had listed some more life cycles connected with me. My gaze locked onto the first lines; and what was written there took my breath away and touched me deeply. She had seen that in a previous incarnation I had lived as a woman of Galilee, and had been in the presence of Jesus during his crucifixion. This struck a deep emotional chord with me, providing an explanation as to why I am so drawn by the image of Jesus, even though I have no affinity for the tenets of the Christian faith.

I probably needed a reminder from Marie that "by chance" I now live in the very land where Jesus lived and acted, which is "by chance" also a land where there are many ancient churches and synagogues whose secrets are waiting to be revealed to me.

6... Music Meets Architecture

My Alsace connection commenced many years ago when my younger brother, Jean-Yves got a job as a contrabass player with the Strasbourg Philharmonic Orchestra. When I visited him, I would always spend hours roaming around the great Cathedral in the city center. I was taken there the first time by a friend of his, also a contrabass player, who sits next to him in the orchestra and is a great fan of the Cathedral. As a youngster, he used to steal in at night and go up to the tower. In this way, he became "acquainted" with one of the watchmen with whom he forged a long-lasting bond of friendship. On my first visit, he introduced me to his friend, who took us to the crypt, which tourists are generally not allowed to enter. Eventually, I made another friend, the curator of the cathedral museum. Whenever I was at the Cathedral, I would map out the place and make a note of the energy levels at various points. I discovered how the properties of the terrain were utilized in order to elevate the spiritual energy level for the benefit of visiting believers. And I read the underlying story of the symbolism of the architectural structure. Did you know, for example, that a cathedral is a great woman lying supine and waiting to be divinely impregnated? The sun shining via the front rosette or rose window blesses the cathedral with its power.

KURSI

I was awaiting an opportunity to visit a site in Israel that would speak to me in that same ancient language of symbols. The opportunity arrived when my brother came for his annual vacation in the summer of 2004 and I took him to Kursi, near Lake Kinneret (the Sea of Galilee). We were directed there by someone who told us that this was a special place; but just how special it was, I had no notion.

Kursi is situated on the eastern shore of Lake Kinneret. It boasts a church and a monastery, with an adjacent bathhouse. These were only discovered in 1970. This combination of church and bathhouse is unique in that it has not been found anywhere else, as far as I know. Archeologists estimated that the first stones of the building were placed in the Fifth Century CE. The nearby hillock is marked as the place where, according to the New Testament, the "miracle of the swine" had occurred. The text has it that Jesus drove the demons out of a possessed man and transferred them to a herd of swine grazing nearby. The swine rushed madly

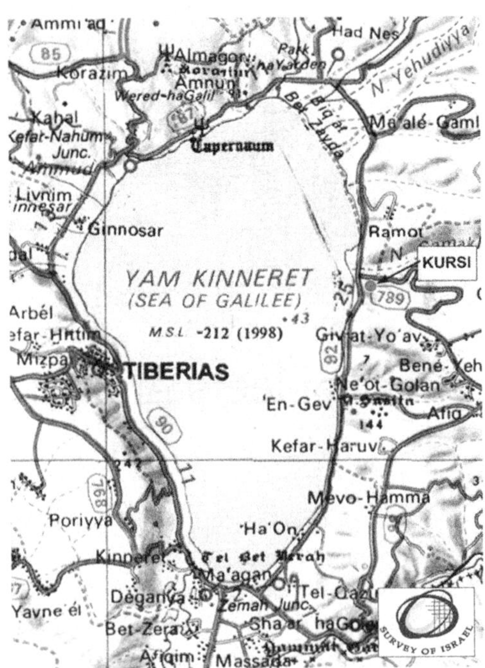

FIG. 7: KURSI - NEXT TO THE SEA OF GALILEE

down the hill and into the Sea of Galilee, where they drowned. While reading about this local history in a leaflet from the Parks Authority, my brother and I entered the park and were inadvertently drawn to a big tree, beneath which were two wooden benches. As we stood facing the benches, I measured the energy level. To my surprise, I had to ratchet higher and higher up the measuring scale until reaching units denominated in the millions. I measured 8 million Bovis at this site! Standing there, I felt as if I were hovering in mid-air. By comparison, the highest energy level I recorded at the Strasbourg Cathedral was 2.5 million Bovis.

FIG. 8: THE CHURCH WITH THE SITE OF THE MIRACLE OF THE SWINE

FIG. 9: ANCIENT RUIN OF A THERMAL BATH

I began examining the features of the terrain, and especially the location of the subterranean waters. Under the bathhouse there are canalization pipes carrying water to be heated. At a depth of 83 meters, there is a subterranean stream with a flow of 600 liters per hour. The current flowed in the direction of the church.

FIG. 10: DISCOVERING A HIGH POINT

Near the church there is an energy-intensive ley line, three meters[1] in width. This line has an energy level of 1.1 million Bovis. Both the stream and the ley line pass beneath the church and are running close to the two benches. Next to the benches, moreover, I discovered what I thought then to be a chimney that was causing the dowsing rods to spin out of control. I marked it in my records as a high energy point. Architecturally speaking, the church had been constructed as a basilica, a style that was widespread in the Fourth and Fifth Centuries CE. Two rows of white marble columns divide the nave into three sections. The columns, with Corinthian capitals, supported stone arches, and remnants of those arches are being reconstructed at the site. The electromagnetic (Hartmann and Curry) lines were moved by the builders so as to pass exactly under the centers of the columns. This use of the electromagnetic networks allowed the energy to run up the columns to the arches above, enveloping the people entering the church. This very same technique was previously used in synagogues in the Land of Israel. The know-how was later passed on to the builders of churches and cathedrals in Europe. The subterranean stream flowing beneath the church passes along the structure's central axis to reach the altar at the rear. At the entrance to the church I measured an energy level of 110,000 Bovis and

---

1. About 9 ft.

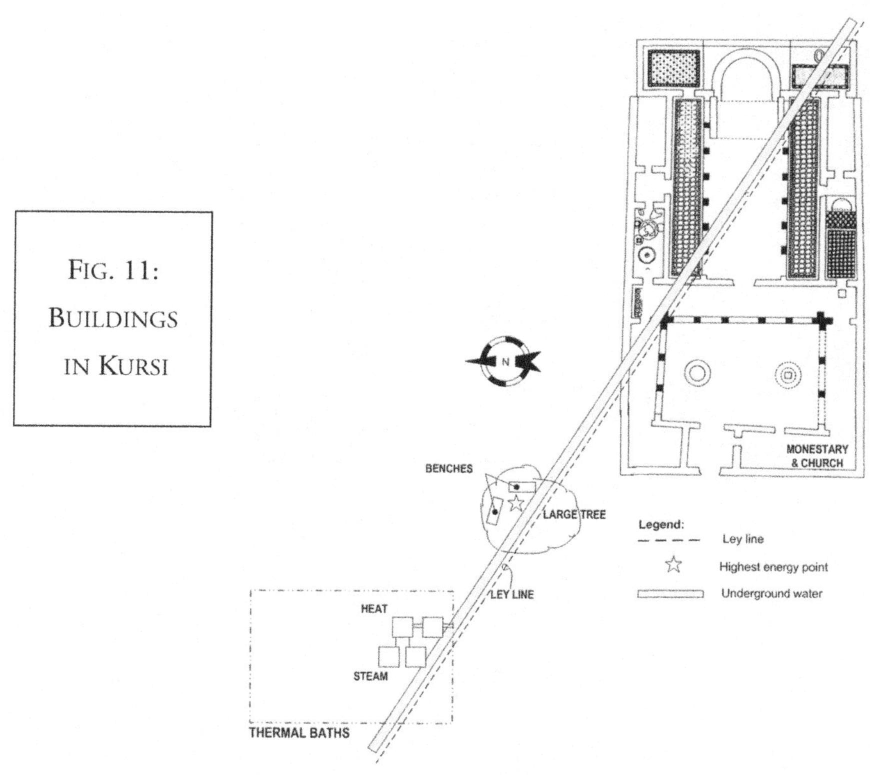

alongside the altar 1.2 million Bovis. Near the altar was a high-energy point, which at that time I took to be a telluric chimney.

This underground stream flowing beneath the bathhouse to the tree and the benches, also reaches the baptismal font, at the rear of the building. I tested the energy level of the font: one million Bovis. By mental activation of the baptismal font I arrived at 2.1 million Bovis. In the past, it would seem, the font was activated by prayers and psalms, thereby charging believers with a great deal of energy.

I had to find out more about this site. A few days after our visit, I called a medium whose channeled communications I find credible. I asked him to find out why this site is so extraordinarily energetic.

He told me that extraterrestrial entities had visited Kursi in the past.

"A gigantic quartz crystal is buried there and has precipitated a great deal of change. Spiritual individuals and persons of high sensitivity came there to charge their energies and heal others. Jesus probably visited the place to charge his own powers and also to heal his followers."

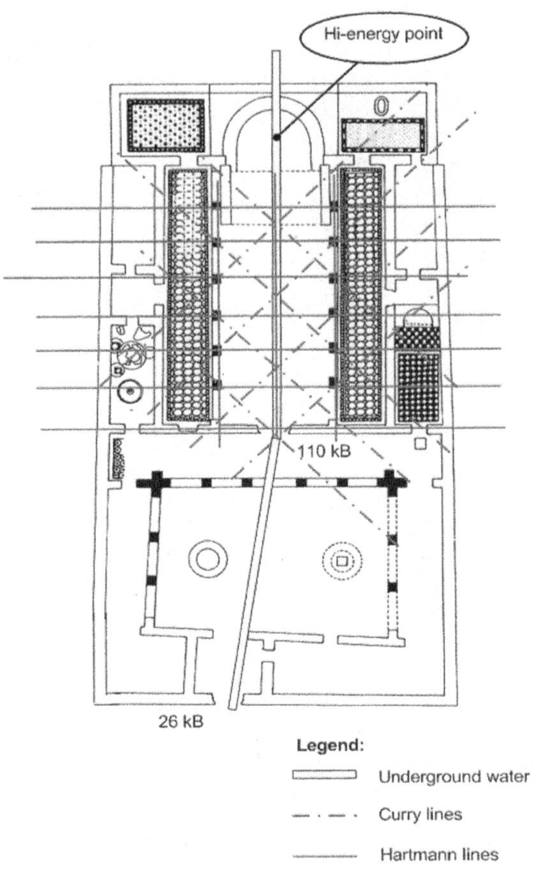

FIG. 12: ENERGETIC MAPPING OF CHURCH

FIG. 13: UNDERGROUND CISTERN IN COURTYARD

FIG. 14: BAPTISTERY

7... The Circles at Rujm-el-Hiri

A mysterious location on the Golan Heights attracts many researchers and scientists. The Arabic name for the place is Rujm-el-Hiri, or "Stone Heap of the Wild Cat." In Hebrew it is called Gilgal Refaim[1], or "Wheel of Refaim." The same root underlies the word used in the Bible to refer to a race of giants, the "Rephaites," described as the ancient people of the Bashan (modern Golan).

Since the discovery of the site in 1967, it has been investigated and measured by means of radar and has been subjected to archeological digging. There are also indications that, for no obvious reason, people shifted things and dug a relatively new pit. Numerous articles have been written about Rujm-el-Hiri, and there's much information about it on the Internet.

---

1. Refa'im in Hebrew means "ghosts" or "spirits."

I was directed there by Shmuel Shaul, a tour guide who practices Egyptian and Hebrew shamanism. He told me that this was one of the most fascinating spots that one could visit. I made a number of fruitless attempts to get there. With rocks and bushes sprouting everywhere, the region is not hiker-friendly. The first time I went looking for the site, my son Tal came along, but our search found nothing. Next time, I went alone, fortified with an excellent map, but again I got nowhere. For my third attempt, in September 2004, I asked for help from some members of the Moshav Yonatan community who lived nearby, which proved worthwhile. I reached the site and found four stone circles; the largest was 150 meters in diameter[1] and consisted of about 42,000 basalt rocks with a large tumulus in the center.

I asked myself why people would erect such a structure. It was obviously a laborious task, necessitating the manual labor of large numbers of workers. Also, the site where they elected to build the stone circles is not particularly accessible. To reach it, you must plod your way over a field of thorn bushes that is full of stones, and then you must ford a stream, which is sometimes quite a difficult task that can only be accomplished by two persons supporting one another. To enter into the outermost circle without climbing the walls, you have to go around and find the north-eastern entrance. Standing at the center involves climbing the tumulus, which is a physically demanding task.

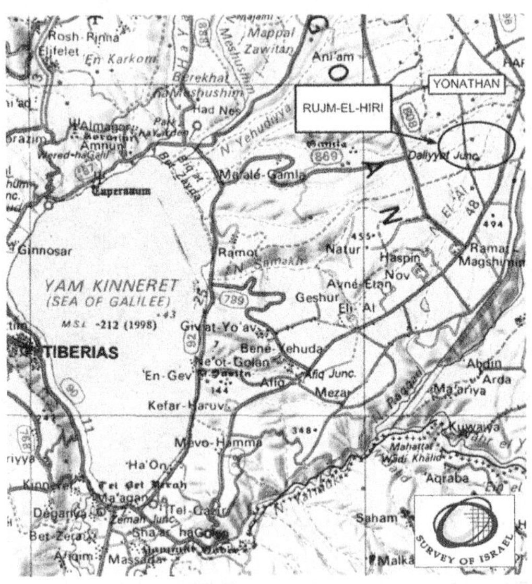

FIG. 15: GEOGRAPHIC LOCATION FOR RUJM-EL-HIRI

Yet I was attracted by the stone-circle configuration—it posed a riddle for me. I proposed to investigate it from a geobiologist's viewpoint, which is to say, to examine its energy profile. Later, I arrived at a clearer understanding of the importance of the place for the Earth's envelope.

The first time I came to Rujm-el-Hiri, I looked at the demarcated area and took measurements. I was amazed at the tremendous size of the place and at

---

1. 492 ft.

how high its energy levels were. Regrettably, I could stay only a few hours; but I was intrigued. What was the place meant for?

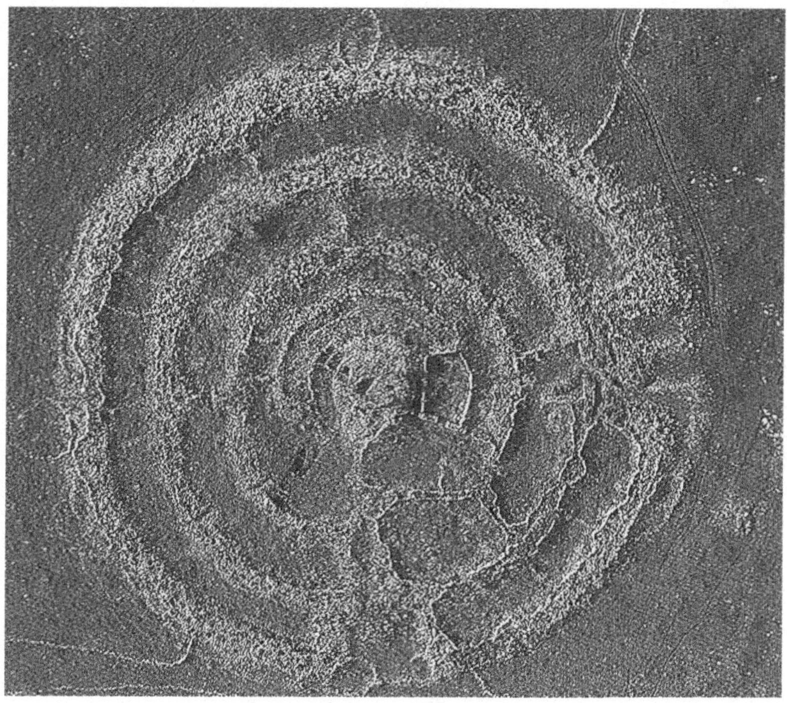

FIG. 16: AERIAL VIEW OF RUJM-EL-HIRI
(COMPLIMENTS OF ITAMAR GREENBURG)

Turning to my medium friend for assistance, I asked what the site had been intended for in the past. The site was indeed very ancient, he replied, and had been in existence for more than 3,000 years. Rujm-el-Hiri, he said, had served as a site of healing. Ceremonies had been conducted there, and offerings had been made in the form of donations and gifts of flowers, fruit and crystals. The stone circles symbolize the gods of the Earth and fertility, and the cyclicality of Nature. Each circle represents either a season of the year or the god responsible for it. People greatly honored and cherished the sacred site and were at pains to render gifts to the gods and entities as a mark of gratitude.

He added that the know-how in accordance with which the site had been built had come from the lore of ancient Babylon. Rujm-el-Hiri is a high-energy site whose water contains minerals that are beneficial for the human body. The water is good for both bathing and drinking. The ceremonies conducted there were originally pagan, but the Jews, too, are known to have come there to be healed of their ills and to seek a blessing. When the site was at the peak of its activity, the ceremonies were conducted by a priestess by the name of Nogia Nogia, which means: "she who touches gods, and gives ancient blessings" (the gods being the Nephilim).

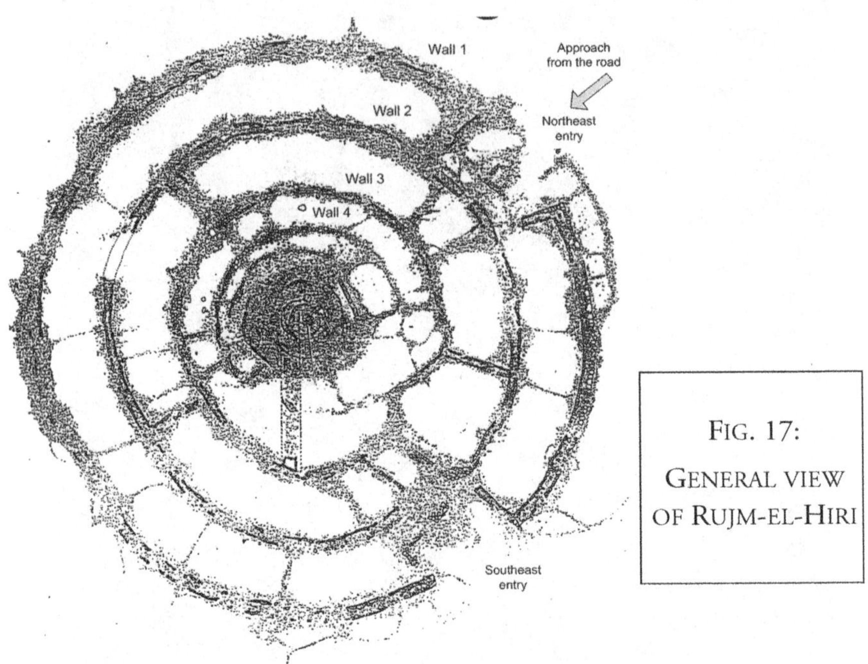

FIG. 17:

GENERAL VIEW OF RUJM-EL-HIRI

The medium had some guidance for visitors coming to the site today: Before entering, you must connect with it spiritually through meditation and ceremony, expressing gratitude and making good wishes. All this must be done in order to generate a positive energy circle whose purpose is to create a blessed future.

Armed with this knowledge, I assumed that, here too, when builders were about to choose a location for a holy site and erect it in accordance with precise rules, they had reckoned with subterranean features—underground water streams, faults, vortices and chimneys. I would surely find such features, I thought, and, indeed, I did.

At the same time, I contacted my good friend Stephane Cardinaux in Switzerland, sending him an aerial photograph of the site. He was glad to assist, and he sent me the following data:

"The contours of the site structure and the physical arrangement of the stones are:

Circle (A), marked around the outermost circle of stones, enables us to draw the other circles by dividing their diameters, one after another, by 1.618, the golden ratio.

Circles (B) are drawn by means of lines tangential to circles (A): tangency lines (trigonometric calculation) at an angle of 58.28º. This angle is created by the diagonal of the golden rectangle.

Circle (C) is tangential to the line that creates an angle of 58.28º to the diameter of big circle (A).

Conclusion: the golden ratio was used in the construction of each of the walls."

Aha! If that is the case, then the circle builders knew a thing or two about Sacred Geometry.

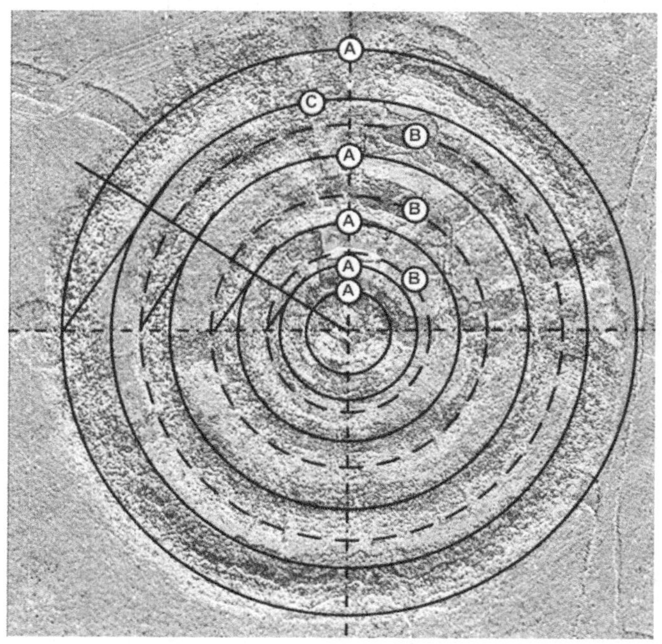

FIG. 18:

GEOMETRIC ANALYSIS OF RUJM-EL-HIRI

We know of use being made of the golden ratio as far back as the art of ancient Egypt. The ancient Egyptians were evidently adept at using mathematics in art, long before the 13th century in which the mathematician Leonardo Fibonacci examined the ratio between two successive terms in a series of integers each of which is equal to the sum of the two preceding terms (the Fibonacci Sequence: 0, 1, 1, 2, 3, 5, 8, 13, 21, 34, 55, 89...).

The ratio he found approximated 1.618. The ancient architects who designed the Great Pyramid in Giza determined that the ratio between the height of the pyramidal wall and half the length of its base would be 1.618.

Four thousand years later, Leonardo da Vinci painted the Mona Lisa. The ratio set by the artist between the width and the length of the face of the image was 1.618. This is also the ratio between the width and the length of the portrait as a whole.

As early as 5100 years ago, structures were being created with an astounding level of accuracy. Consider, for example, an ancient structure discovered in Morbihan in France in 1963, in which all the dimensions of the structure are based on the golden ratio of 1.618, as are all the angles. And to cap it all, the different dimensions create a Fibonacci sequence.

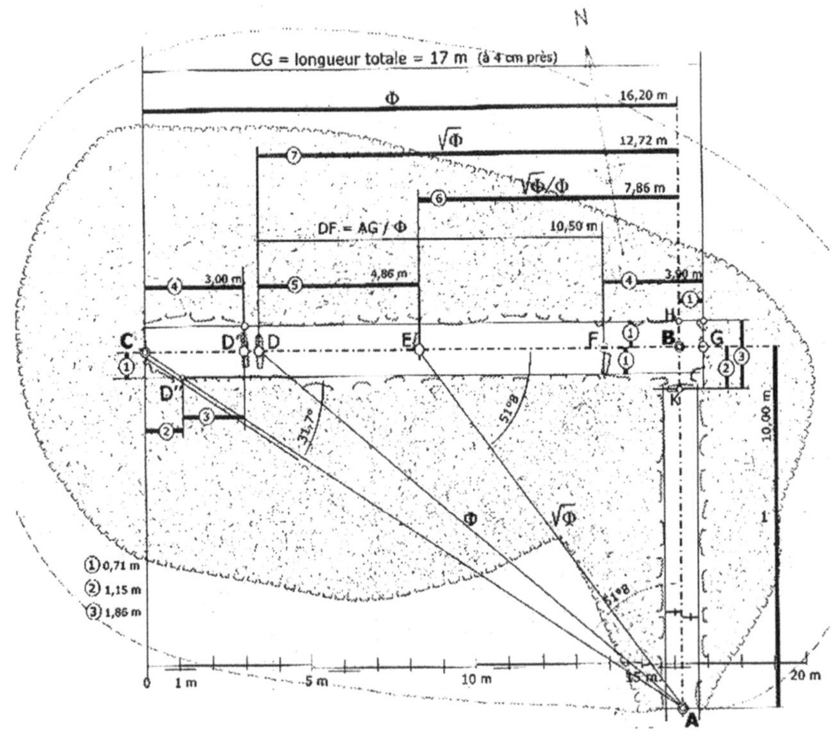

FIG. 19: THE GOLDEN RATIO AT MORBIHAN IN FRANCE

In any event, we must bear in mind that in the past, the measuring devices we have today were not available. Measurements have been taken at many sites without any reference whatsoever to the golden ratio. For example, Alexander Thom, who discovered the stone circle at Borrowston Rig in Scotland, which is about 4,500 years old, took precise measurements of the site, and made no connection with the golden ratio.

To assess the energy levels at Rujm-el-Hiri, I took measurements at each circle and in between the circles. The closer a person approaches to the center, the higher the energy levels are. Ultraviolet vibrations are very high, among other things, due to the circular shape of the site. The vibration planes cover the entire spectrum, ranging from the mental at the first circle, to the divine at the central circle directly around the tumulus. There is a gradual increase here showing both the rise of the energies themselves and the improvement in their quality.

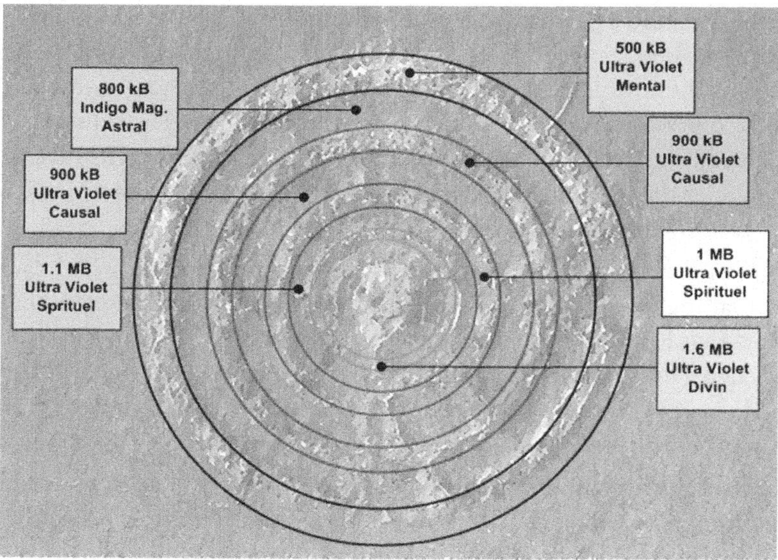

FIG. 20: ENERGETIC MAPPING OF RUJM-EL-HIRI

I also looked for any similarity between the structure of Rujm-el-Hiri and other structures with which I was already acquainted. When investigating ancient churches and synagogues in Israel and France, I noted that they were similar in architecture and positioning, starting with the underground structure and its geological properties. In all instances, the central hall or nave is invariably positioned above a fault, and sometimes over a subterranean stream (in which case, a wet fault). Moreover, if the fault changes direction at any point, the building follows suit.

At Rujm-el-Hiri I looked for and found a subterranean stream. The current moves from west to east, with a width of 2.1 meters,[1] and it flows at a depth of 33 meters[2] at a rate of flow of 5.3 cubic meters per hour.[3] Apart from

---

1. 6 ft. 10 in.

the subterranean current, there is also a fault 6.7 meters[1] wide at a depth of 51 meters. When one stands in the midpoint of the subterranean stream, about 10 meters outside the outermost wall, the energy level is 4,000 Bovis, as could be expected. As I approached the wall, the energy level rose rapidly. At a distance of two meters away, the energy level reached 100,000 Bovis.

The underlying secret of this high energy level is its shape. Countless stones in a configuration of concentric circles engender a change in the energy phase and level. This phenomenon is widespread in consecrated buildings: the water energy outside up to the periphery of the structure is negative; but the moment one enters the structure, the building form itself exerts an influence such that the energy becomes positive. At Rujm, on the eastern side, where the water exits the structure, the energy level is very high, even at a great distance from the outermost wall. I was unable to measure the level at a distance of more than 20 meters[2] from the wall, due to a fence bearing signs that warned the public of the presence of buried mines. Yet even at that point, the energy level was 900,000 Bovis.

Standing next to the eastern fence, I noticed a distant hill with a large antenna at the top. On the basis of what I had learned in previous instances, I assumed that Rujm-el-Hiri had an energetic link to the hill; and sure enough, I found such a link 1.5 meters[3] wide. The link had an energy level of 1.1 million Bovis. I thought it would be interesting, some time in the future, to examine the distant hill as well.

Seemingly by chance, the subject of energy links surfaced in my memory. I had a flickering recall of such links being found in France and no doubt elsewhere as well, especially between small and large churches and between one village and another one nearby. Only later would I understand the significance of energy links between sites with high energy levels. That would happen once I obtained a perspective on the expansive system that creates the energetic web enveloping the terrestrial globe, and once I was able to grasp its significance and understand how it works. All this would become clear to me only when I learned what role my work was to play as part of the global set-up.

2. 108 ft.
3. 187 cu. ft./hr.
1. 22 ft.
2. 66 ft.
3. 5 ft.

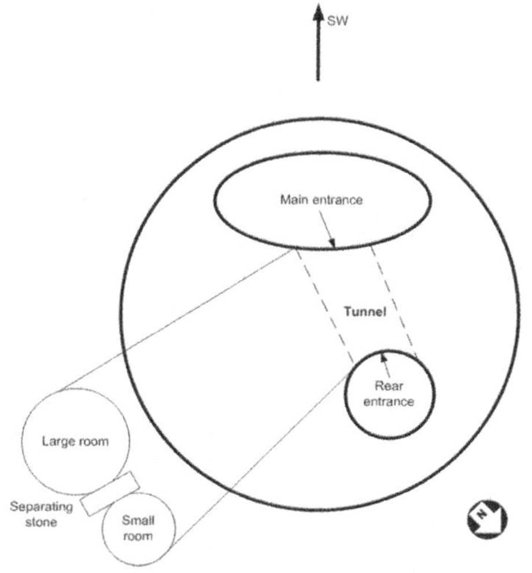

FIG. 21:
SCHEMATIC
REPRESENTATION OF THE
TUMULUS

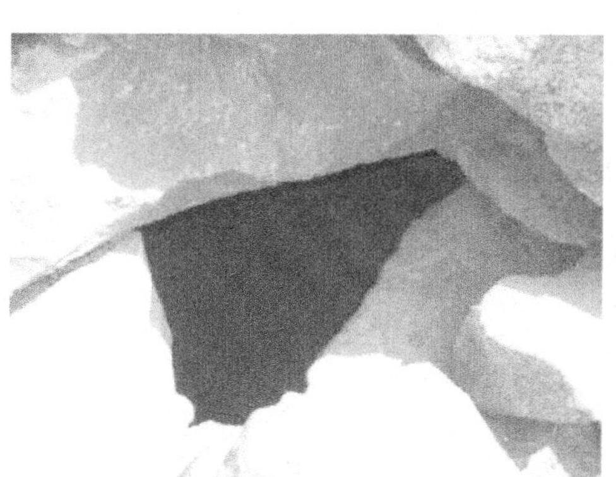

FIG. 22: MAIN ENTRANCE OF
THE TUMULUS

FIG. 23: INSIDE THE
LARGE ROOM

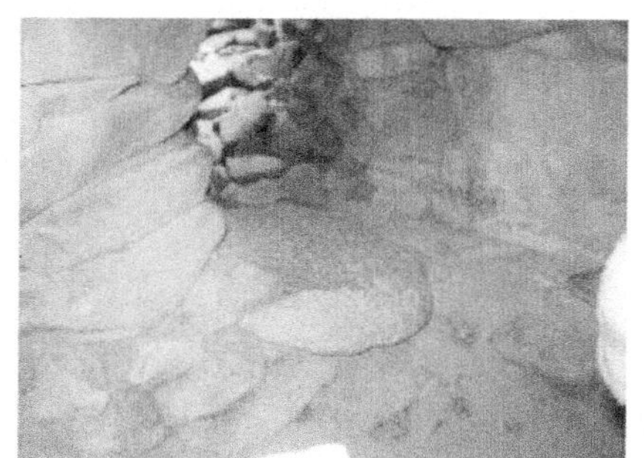

FIG. 24: LARGE, SEPARATING STONE

FIG. 25: REAR ENTRANCE

8... Arise and Walk the Land

One day I offered to my new friend Géèma to come with me to visit Kursi, so that I could show him the exceptional energy phenomenon and we could investigate the theory of the existence of the big quartz crystal (as reported to me by the medium I had approached after my first visit). Géèma, as I have indicated, is knowledgeable about geobiology and is also able to communicate with energetic entities and channel their messages spontaneously. Apart from that, he has a unique talent for seeing the invisible. So off we went. He began by measuring the energy level at the location of the two benches. His results confirmed the measurements I had taken there three-and-a-half years earlier. Then he sat on the rock alongside the benches and commenced writing spontaneously in French, while staying mentally in contact with his source ("the Family"). The following is what he wrote during this channeling session:

"You are now present at a center of revitalization of a Lemurian town that can only be seen in the fifth dimension. Richard, who is with you, first discovered this site 2000 years ago. Richard was then one of the followers of Jesus: a woman by the name of Yohanna.[1]

Five crystals are located in Kursi. The central crystal obtains energies from the other four. Each crystal channels a different type of energy; and when these energies merge with the energy of the central crystal[2] they generate a sacred, cosmic energy.

In this site there is a building which is not visible because it is in another dimension, roofed with a dome and divided into various rooms. The Lemurians, when they come to rest over the central crystal, enjoy rejuvenation. In the fifth dimension, time is meaningless, and even if their body is made of corporeal matter, that matter is far lighter than that of the human body. On this plane, there is absolute control over the exchange between matter and energy and vice versa. This control endows them with perfect health and prevents aging.

They are also capable of teleportation. Before the year 2012, you will encounter your Lemurian brothers, who are looking forward, impatiently, to that moment."

I heard all this with great excitement and enthusiasm. This was the first time I had been present while my friend was channeling. Eager to put the information to use there and then, I looked to find where the crystals were located, and to measure the distance between them. For the purpose of the search I used a pendulum and a pair of telescopic antennas. Relying on the fact that the peripheral crystals were linked to the central crystal, I sought the connecting line farther and farther away from the center. Then I went back along the energy line until I located the exact placement of the crystal.

Later, at home, I made an illustration in which I marked out five locations, each indicating the placement of one of the crystals, its depth and the planet from which it had arrived (since Géèma had said that each of them came from a different planet).

---

1. In French, the name came out as Johanna, but the Hebrew pronunciation is Yokhanna, —R.B
2. It is located beneath the rock opposite the two benches.—R.B

Incidentally, there is no point digging in the hope of finding the crystals—they only exist in the fifth dimension!

The new details that were divulged to me through the channeling session also left me with a great many questions. The Kursi site, then, is well-known thanks to the story of the miracle of the swine in the time of Jesus. And the strong attraction that drew me there in the first place is explained by my previous incarnation as a woman by the name of Yohanna, which I'll explain more later. But there is a far more ancient occult story that relates to the crystals buried there by the Lemurians. The mention of Lemuria, struck a chord with my experience at the workshop in the desert, when I sat by myself on the mound of sand and connected to something deep inside me.

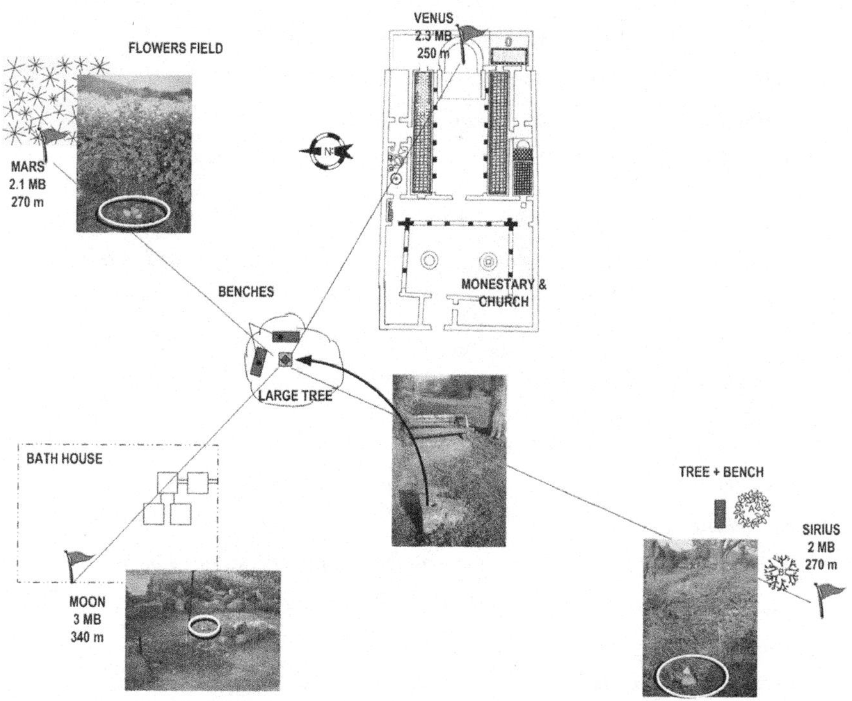

FIG. 26: LOCATIONS OF CRYSTALS

Lemuria was an ancient civilization that had existed both before and during the time of Atlantis. It is believed to have been situated in the southern Pacific Ocean, between North America and Asia-Australia. Lemuria is sometimes also called *Mu* or the *Mother Continent*. In the days of Lemuria's greatest glory, its denizens were highly developed, both physically and spiritually. Even though it is hard to find tangible evidence of this ancient civilization, many people, including myself, sense a close affinity for the Lemurians.

These people, who are connected to Lemuria in such a way that even today they can access the ancient lore, believe that over a long period of time prior to the fall of consciousness (which happened when Atlantis sank), the Lemurians lived in the fifth dimension, and could switch at will between it and the third dimension. They could do this on a moment's whim, by means of intention and the energies of the heart.

To get back to earth, Géèma and I, after spending the morning in Kursi, continued on to Rujm-el-Hiri. But a small stream blocked our way and we could not reach the site (we later discovered that this had been no happenstance or meaningless obstacle). We got back in the car and Géèma once more started taking dictation from "the Family."

Before you is what may be described as "the perfect point" – the center, and offshoots of the center in the form of concentric circles.[1] It is true that various interpretations are placed upon the nature of the site.

Even though its energy levels are lower than that of the site[2] you visited today, this is still a highly energetic site, and an energy hub for the healing of the sick. At first, living quarters were established here. After that, the shamans of this pagan civilization noticed that a great many diseases were erupting among their people and even among livestock.

The shamans established[3] connections to trace the source of the diseases and as a result circular walls around this perfect point, in accordance with guidelines that were given to them. The perfect point may be conceived as a chakra of the Earth, for this area. The results were extraordinarily successful, and it became a regular practice to make offerings to these circles, which were deemed to be spirits. Each season, offerings were made to different spirits. Many years later, invaders destroyed the site and forbade its occupation. The new settlers never knew why circular structures of such perfect geometry had been built or for what purpose. They used the circles for whatever

---

1. Like a pebble that creates ripples when tossed into a lake, —R.B.
2. Kursi —R.B.
3. [spiritual]—R.B

purpose came to mind, and especially to protect their families and domestic animals from threats of local invaders.

The place is not intended for profit-making uses: It must be open and accessible for the esoteric study of occult or sacred realms of knowledge, and for people suffering from respiratory diseases. The site should neither be repaired nor rehabilitated; leave it as is, because there are things that must not be exposed and must not be altered by mistake. Come back to visit the site in the future, because certain energies are slated to change.

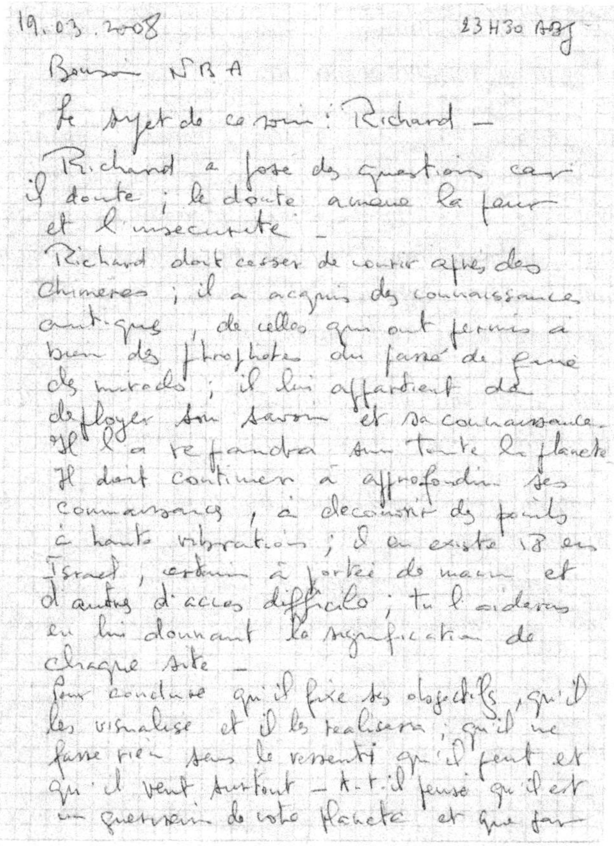
19.03.2008 23H30 ABJ

Bonsoir NBA

Le sujet de ce soir : Richard —

Richard a posé des questions car il doute ; le doute amène la peur et l'insécurité —

Richard doit cesser de courir après des chimères ; il a acquis des connaissances antiques, de celles qui ont permis à bien des prophètes du passé de faire des miracles ; il lui appartient de déployer son savoir et sa connaissance. Il l'a répandra sur toute la planète

Il doit continuer à approfondir ses connaissances, à découvrir des points à hautes vibrations ; il en existe 18 en Israël, certains à portée de main et d'autres d'accès difficile ; tu l'aideras en lui donnant la signification de chaque site —

Pour conclure qu'il fixe des objectifs, qu'il les visualise et il les réalisera ; qu'il ne fasse rien sans le ressenti qu'il peut et qu'il veut surtout — A-t-il pensé qu'il est un guerrier de cette planète et que par—

9... The Mission

A few weeks after our excursion to the north, when we visited Kursi and Rujm-el-Hiri, I paid a call on my friend Géèma at his home. Our shared experiences had been so exciting I could think of nothing else. I had a million questions and things I had been pondering upon and I wanted explanations. Sharing my curiosity, Géèma took a pencil and paper and started taking dictation from the "Family." It was at this meeting that I first got a clue as to what was being asked of me.

Richard asks questions because he is skeptical, but doubt is accompanied by fear and insecurity. He has acquired ancient know-how which in the past enabled prophets to work miracles; it is his duty to disseminate his know-how over the entire planet. He must go on with his in-depth learning and discover Israel's 18 energy-intensive sites, some of which are within reach, while others are harder to access. You will help him by providing the significance of each site.

To conclude, he must establish his objectives, visualize them and he will achieve them. May he do nothing unless he feels able and especially willing to do it. Has it ever occurred to him that he can heal your planet and that by using his mental, he can do things on which the nations of the world cannot reach consensus, in spite of the agreements known as the Kyoto agreements?

Richard must weave with other geobiologists a "cloth" that will be beneficial for the Earth and the Earth will pay them back.

We bless him through you and connect him to the emerald ray that will grant him healing energies, enabling him to find a cure for problems, together with his brothers, scattered across the planet. Extraterrestrials, Lemurians and other entities will help him do this.

Be blessed,

Your Family

Back home, I set about trying to digest all the information that had landed on me. I realized that the trips I believed to have been some random initiative on my part—taking me to Kursi and Rujm-el-Hiri—had in fact marked the beginning of a journey whose significance had yet to become fully apparent to me. I understood that I had somehow been enlisted in service for the benefit of the Earth. I wondered whether I might be biting off more than I could chew; but Géèma's words plucked at a chord deep down in my soul, arousing me to the awareness that this was the most important thing in my life—my true destiny—to act for the good of others, to heal, and to create harmony and peace. I recalled that night in the desert when I became aware of my huge debt to Mother Earth, and the emotional promise I had uttered to dedicate my life to her service.

10... Yohanna

As a first stage in processing these seething emotions, I set out to discover just exactly who Yohanna was. To my surprise, I found she was a known, actual historical figure. She turned out to have been the granddaughter of a man by the name of Jonathan Ben Ananus (Theophilus) who was a High Priest in the Temple in Jerusalem, around 37–41 BCE. Jonathan's father, Ananus, served as a High Priest for the ten-year period 6–15 BCE.

Jewish tradition has it that Jonathan was a direct descendant of Moses' brother Aaron, a member of the Sadducees, a Jewish sect founded in the second century BCE. The Sadducees were the rivals of the Pharisees, who later became the centrist stream that has accompanied us to the present day. The Sadducees, meanwhile, have vanished from off the face of the earth.

Beside this, Theophilus was also the brother-in-law of Yosef Bar Keyfa who grew up in the Temple. This same "Joseph Caiaphas" as he is called in Greek, was responsible for handing Jesus over to the Roman governor Pontius Pilate, who sought to have him executed on charges of rebellion against Rome.

Yohanna was married to Chuza, who served as Herod's right-hand and dealt with his economic interests. The marriage of Yohanna and Chuza was solemnized in accordance with all the customary rites, as they are performed today. The prenuptial agreement in those days assured monetary compensation in case of divorce or death of one of the spouses.

Since she came of a priestly family, Yohanna was allotted a greater amount of compensation. Moreover, at the time of the betrothal, the families had to reach agreement concerning wedding presents. It was decided that the gifts presented by Chuza's father were to go to Yohanna. The gifts traditionally belonged to Yohanna and she might do as she pleased with her property. She helped Jesus and his apostles out of her own means rather than her husband's money.

So the New Testament relates, in Luke 8:1-3:

> *And it came to pass thereafter that Jesus traveled about from one town and village to another, proclaiming the good news of the kingdom of God (Luke 8:1a). Twelve were with him, and also some women who had been cured of evil spirits and diseases: Mary (called Magdalene) from whom seven demons had come out; Yohanna the wife of Chuza, the manager of Herod's household; Susanna; and many others. These women were helping to support Jesus and his disciples out of their own means.*

Having resolved to follow Jesus, Yohanna abandoned Herod's royal court along with her husband Chuza, thus forfeiting both her privileged position and her economic security. She began serving those who in the past had served her.

Yohanna is said to have played a part in the narrative of the death of John the Baptist. This is a story that shows her to have been a kind-hearted woman who was karmically linked with both John the Baptist and Jesus. After Jesus was baptized, Herod Antipas sent John to prison in the fortress palace of Machaerus. John had openly accused Herod of abandoning his wife, daughter of the Nabatean King Aretas IV, in order to cohabit with his brother's wife, Herodias.

On his birthday, Herod held a banquet for his high officials, friends and military commanders. Salome, daughter of Herodias, danced before Herod and his guests. Herod, who greatly enjoyed her dancing, promised to grant any wish she might make. On her mother's advice, Salome requested the head of John the

Baptist, on a platter. Deeply distressed but bound by having given his word, Herod sent a guard to cut the head of John the Baptist. Salome took the platter bearing the saint's severed head, and presented it to her mother, Herodias, who buried it in a place of defilement. But Yohanna removed the head from its impure burial place, placed it in an earthenware vessel, and reburied it on the Mount of Olives, where Herod had a plot. Religious tradition has it that the head of John the Baptist lies in Samaria at a spot where the Crusaders built a church in his memory. In the course of time, the church became a mosque. It is also believed that the head was taken by the Templars, to France, as an object of worship.

Again, Yohanna risked her life by the very act of being present at the crucifixion of Jesus. Only women were left surrounding the dead body of Jesus, for his disciples had long since fled. Yohanna stayed by his side until he was buried. Three days later, together with Mary Magdalene and Susanna, she discovered that Jesus' tomb was empty.

The New Testament relates in Luke 24, 9 – 10:

> *and returned from the tomb and reported all these things to the eleven and to all the rest. Now they were Mary Magdalene and Yohanna and Mary the mother of James; also the other women with them were telling these things to the apostles"*

During one of the many persecutions suffered by the early Christians, Yohanna was imprisoned with her son and other followers of Jesus and taken to the Colosseum in Rome. There on August 27, year 68, she was sacrificed by being burnt on a pyre stake together with her son and several other martyrs who refused to renounce their faith.

Now that I had connected with the story of Yohanna, a message was channeled by the "Family" informing me that in addition to my having been Yohanna in the time of Jesus, I was also a descendant of the Prophet Isaiah who for 40 years had prophesied the destruction of Judea and Israel and the future advent of Jesus. Following this message, the "Family" always called me *Yohanna*, or *Son of the Prophet Isaiah*. What surfaces in this context, interestingly enough, is my original surname. In Algeria, our family name was *Benichou*, which definitely bears a certain resemblance to that of Jesus (ben = son and ichou = Yesus; thus Benichou = son of Jesus). It was only on immigrating to Israel that I Hebraized my name to Benishai, itself a distinguished name, referring to King David who was the son of Ishai, a name that is heavily laden with historic and biblical background. Again, Benishai = son of Isaiah.

In July, Géèma got another message, this one spelling out the task of finding the 18 sites and specifying how Géèma and I were to collaborate. The following are some important extracts:

In recent months, you have been delving into geobiology due to your encounter with Yohanna. He was directed to you and a common frequency was generated between you, dovetailing perfectly with what both of you are doing; each one complementing the other's domain; each understanding and accepting what the other does. Bear in mind the chain of events starting with the meeting in Abidjan through Kursi and so forth... these visits to the holy places were no coincidence.

The energy mix between you, yours and that of Yohanna, has created a third frequency, one that resonates with ours.

We have indicated 18 sites in Israel, but we must tell you that the number 18 represents only a part of the high-energy sites in Israel. But this is sufficient to integrate the country into the region to which it belongs. For us, the Earth is a major entity, divided into energy zones and not into countries whose borders may be modified at the whim of man or history. Israel belongs to the region of the Middle East, riding on two continents. There are another four, with a total of five regions altogether; this is not relevant for you, because you can only work in your own country; go on with your searches and activate vortices and chimneys.

Earth is an entity whose energetic body consists of capillaries, veins and arteries. The Earth also has organs that are nourished by cosmic energy, some of it reaching you in the form of telluric energy. The Earth, like a body, moves (to your regret), but breathes (fortunately for you).

We see that you are making an effort to understand what you are supposed to do. We send you bits of information that are not always comprehensible to you, Yohanna. But Géèma does, after all, understand. He has had access to the fourth dimension, which prepared him for additional missions.

We want to put before you[1] certain explanations concerning what you are doing and what may be expected to happen. The earth is enclosed in a lattice, like a blanket, with spaces between the threads. The activation of what you refer to as vortices and chimneys restores the equilibrium of the loops of the blanket. It is difficult for us to make ourselves understood, because we speak a technical language that, for the present, is foreign to you; and we prefer to let you make discoveries and do your own investigating.

A comparison may help you to understand what we are saying: you readjust the currents passing through the capillaries, veins and arteries and thereby invigorate them, without preventing the flow of energies. When the rate and pressure of the energy flow are good, the pipelines become transparent and then you are able to see the colors of the different energies. Believe me: they are marvelously beautiful; these are our Las Vegas lights.

We love and admire you and have been at your side for thousands of years. We have always known you, and we are aware of all your doings, past and present. As for the future — that is a matter of free will. Know that we are with you in the work you are doing now and will continue to do. Because you are doing what we cannot: this work, which is a co-creation with Spirit, with God, puts you in a good place, and we express our appreciation for it. Even if you are not always aware of what you are doing, the day will come when you will know. And, there will be great celebrations.

---

1. Yohanna - R.B.

11... High-Energy Sites

I began a search for the other sites. My method of searching was no ordinary one, since it was based on listening intuitively to messages that reached me from various sources. Information frequently came from my geobiology students, who would point to this or that place (many of them being connected with Spirit) and in that way I created a list of sites to be investigated. I had great faith that I was being guided in such a way as to ensure that I reached the right places. I methodically traced the points with the aid of maps and satellite photographs on the Internet, magnifying them until I could actually see the terrain surface. When I found a site with a positive and especially high energy level, I set out to discover its energy "story."

One of these places was Avdat, a Nabataean town in the Negev.

Avdat

In its present location, Avdat was built as an assembly point for the many caravans that crossed the paths of the Negev desert. Avdat was founded in the first century BCE by the Nabateans, a Semitic people living in the Negev, in Edom and in Transjordan from the third century BCE until the seventh century CE. Originally, they had been nomads, becoming merchants in the course of time and leading caravans along the Spice Road —ancient paths for the trading caravans that carried spices from the Arabian Peninsula to the lands of the Mediterranean. They established six towns in the Negev. They left no written evidence behind, but are mentioned in various Greek and Latin sources.

The town has a temple and public buildings that could be seen from a distance and served as a landmark for those travelling with the caravan. Avdat was meant to be

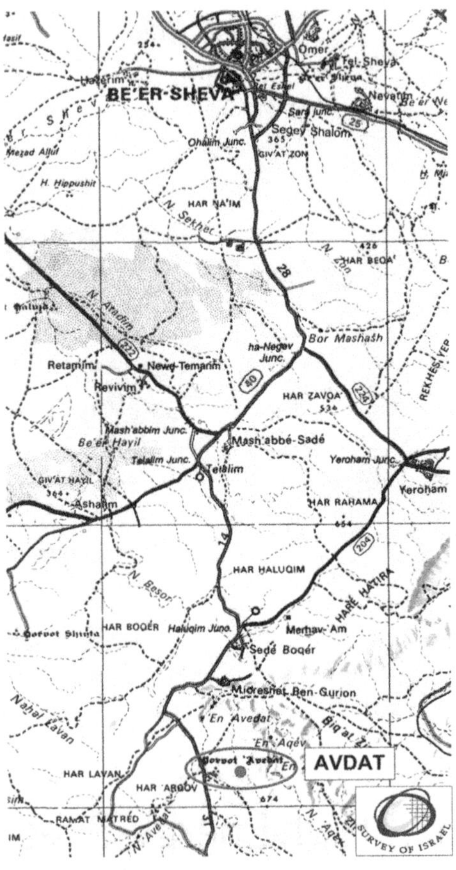

Fig. 27: Location of Avdat

a place of rest and recreation. The weary travelers could find respite from the travails of the road, and gather the strength to go on with their journey. The Nabateans were experts at water storage. Along the roads, they concealed countless reservoirs known only to them, so that they could survive throughout their incessant wanderings. In settled communities, they built a system of canals to gather and store whatever small quantities of rainfall came their way. In this way, they were able to sustain agriculture in arid places.

I set off for Avdat on a particularly hot day; but the dryness prevailing in the Negev makes the heat relatively tolerable. I was hoping my son Tal would join me, and I recalled how pleasant it was when we made our way to Rujm-el-Hiri together. At the time, Tal was studying at the nearby Ben Gurion College.

As it turned out, he was unable to join me that day. So be it —I continued on my own.

FIG. 28: AERIAL PHOTO OF AVDAT

I started looking for the various features I had found in the aerial photograph of Avdat on which I had done some preparatory work at home. I found a chimney that was actually located on the threshold of the winery. The presence of a chimney there would certainly have had a beneficial effect on the wine being produced. From that point, I sought and found the links to the two other chimneys that I already knew existed. One was at the very edge of the cliff. I was not surprised to discover that the circumference of the chimney was elliptical – I had seen this shape on the chimneys on Mt. Tabor and elsewhere.

After my first trip to Avdat, I asked Géèma to hold a channeling session concerning the place and the work I had done so far. The channeling session spoke of the people who had worked at Avdat in ancient times:

In the olden days, people communicated amongst themselves by foot-trekking or by riding beasts of burden. Generally speaking, a journey of ten or more days would be required before men, women and children could find a place to rest, renew their strength, water the parched cells of their bodies, eat and sleep. Avdat was one of the way stations. Sometimes, the nomads would set out on such journeys with their families, and it would happen that they did not return to the same place until several years later.

By using their mental powers, they created a site with high energies, not only to rehabilitate themselves physically, but also so that each one could connect to his or her higher self. Asleep at night, they would pass to other planes, in which they found solutions to their problems. By connecting regularly in such as way, they generated ecumenical thought patterns, resulting from all the beliefs and the various religions of the travelers gathering there. The main idea was to be connected to the supreme Being residing in each of us.

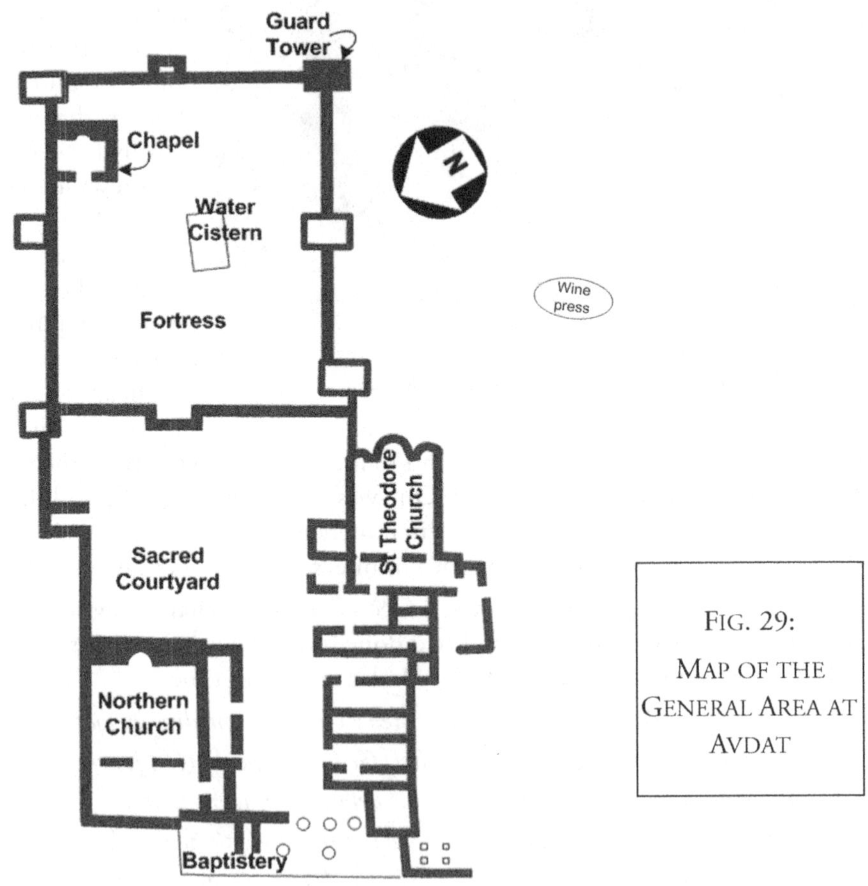

FIG. 29:

MAP OF THE GENERAL AREA AT AVDAT

The energy measured at the site originates from the residual memories of past happenings, leaving their imprint on earth and rocks. This triangle [1] is an area of healing for those suffering from general frailty

---

1. Formed by the three chimneys, —R.B.

*and poor health. Such people must come here. You will be surprised
how quickly their power will regenerate.*

*We recommend setting up an infrastructure here where the sick can
spend the night, because the work of renewal takes place primarily by
night. Avdat is part of the 18 high-energy sites. Each of the 18 sites
has a unique healing power. The development of this site will gain
impetus by means of your writings and your search. Define and mark
the exact locations.[1] Somebody will latch on to this idea, will bring it
to fruition and set up the infrastructure.*

In light of the recommendation that had come through the channeling
session, I returned to Avdat about a month later, this time together with my
son Tal. We were searching for the exact location of the three chimneys, so that
they could be marked on the map. I located the three chimneys, and together
we began measuring the distances.

"Why don't you look for other chimneys?" Tal asked. As I have already
remarked, when suggestions of this sort come my way, I treat them as a message
that needs to be looked into. My son may have received a hint from the
"Family." I carried on searching, and sure enough, I found another three
chimneys.

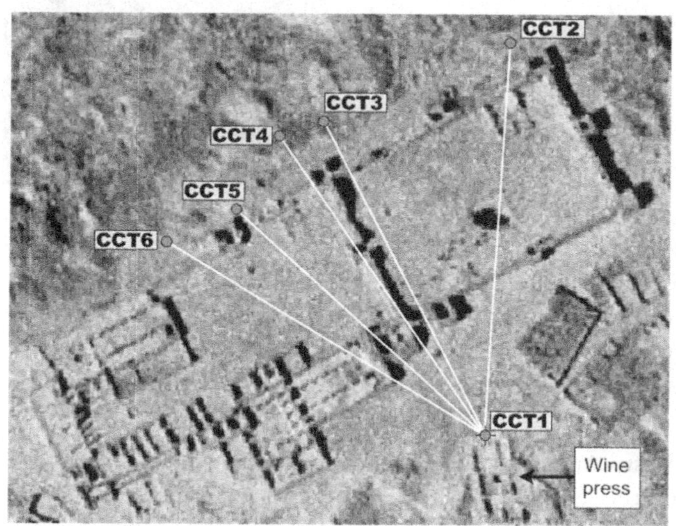

FIG. 30:

LOCATION OF
THE CHIMNEY
NETWORK AT
AVDAT

---

1. Of the chimneys —R.B.

This time, I performed a check and noted on my drawings certain additional elements such as underground faults and water currents. I used dowsing rods to seek out the electromagnetic networks (Hartmann and Curry). What I discovered were "greetings" from the past, from those of the site's builders who had been fully aware that they could make use of the energy lines to meet the needs of visitors.

Some electromagnetic lines can be found at the main entrance to the site. Since the entire building was erected at an angle of 45° north-east, the lines that pass beneath the main entrance belong to the Curry network. To create a multiplicity of densely woven lines, the builders used a mental process called de-multiplication. In this mental process, a single Curry line is split into several lines, some of the lines—usually within the building—rendered positive while the rest, adjacent to the outer wall of the building, made to be negative.

FIG. 31: VIEW OF THE VALLEY THROUGH THE MAIN ENTRANCE

This arrangement which, later on, was also instituted in churches and cathedrals, enables the energies of whoever passes the church threshold to be cleansed. Thus, people arriving from far away and who carried negative (or positive) energies, were cleansed and disrobed of them before entering into the holy place.

An underground stream also flows through the main entrance. Interestingly enough, the width of the stream is exactly the same as that of the entrance. This fact hints that it has not changed direction in two thousand years; it is possible, however, that there is no longer any water flow, and that what I measured was merely a memory of water.

Near the main entrance is another entrance that leads to the churchyard. At this entrance too, a stream of water is combined below ground, with a subterranean fault that continues the whole length of the site. Standing above the current, I measured an energy level of 220,000 Bovis.

The water flowed from the rear to the front of the site. The fault was 50 cm wide, with an energy level of 60,000 Bovis. Similar geobiological phenomena are to be found in more or less ancient structures in various places. In Egypt, for example, the Temple of Luxor was built in such a way that its longitudinal axis would run parallel to an underground fault lying beneath it. Also, the Cathedral of Notre Dame in Paris was built parallel to a subterranean fault line. Accordingly, the plans of both buildings indicate that they are crooked—Notre Dame being slightly askew and Luxor distinctly off-center.

In the southern part of the site is the Church of St. Theodor. Built in the fifth century CE, it was dedicated to the fourth-century Greek martyr, by that name. It boasts two rows of columns positioned over Curry and Hartmann lines, as can be found in later churches. Here I found further confirmation that the people of that time were already aware of the existence of subterranean energies and electromagnetic grids, and knew how to utilize them for their own benefit. The energy level at the altar was around 430,000 Bovis.

FIG. 32: ENTRANCE TO THE SACRED COURTYARD

Later on, I was to discover two sites that connect to Avdat to create an energy structure that will operate in constant flow. But at this stage, I first had to go on discovering additional sites in the north.

FIG. 33: FRONT VIEW OF THE CHURCH OF ST. THEODOR

12... The Secret of Longevity

I was staying in Abidjan, on one of my trips to the Ivory Coast, when I got a call from a "Maariv" newspaper reporter, who said he had been referred to me by one of my students, Yael Berkovitz from kibbutz Nir David. It seems that a very high percentage of the elderly people living on the kibbutz were in their nineties; and some were even centenarians. When he tried to find out why, Yael sent him to me.

My off-the-cuff reply was, "The kibbutz may have been built above a place where there is no underground water flow." It stands to reason that a rare event of this type could come about. My experience has shown, time after time, that the greatest damage to our health derives from the negative effect of underground water flows. Could this kibbutz somehow have been sited over a dry patch? Shortly after that, the reporter published an article titled: "The Kibbutz Where People Don't Die"—sensational enough, for sure.

On returning to Israel, I took the time to look into the matter more closely. My first move was to inspect the kibbutz by means of aerial photographs. I examined the energy variables for the entire kibbutz. I found the vibration level to stand at 25,000 Bovis. This is comparable to the energy usually found in a private home once I have blocked the energies of the underground currents. Did this imply that there were no underground water currents beneath the kibbutz?

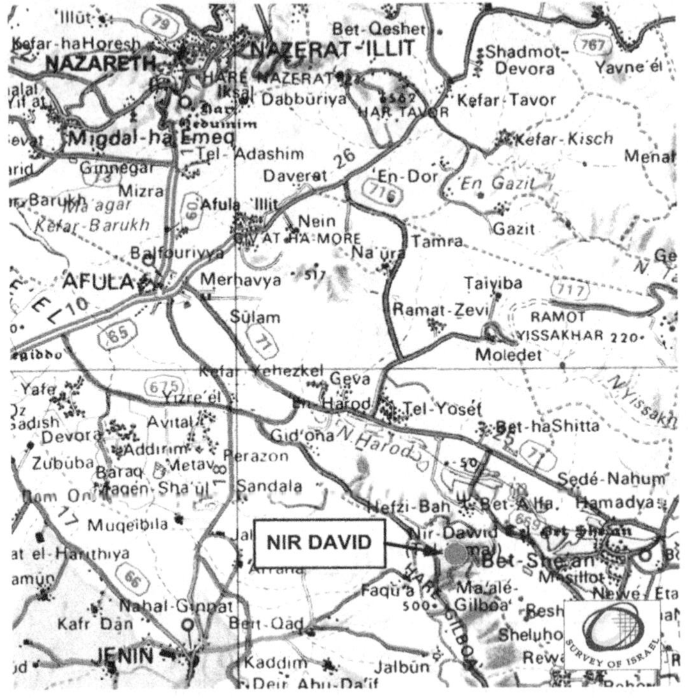

FIG. 34: GEOGRAPHICAL LOCATION FOR NIR DAVID

Correspondingly, there was a 90% magnetic-field effect. This almost perfect result is likewise consistent with the vibration level and is usually obtained following blockage of the negatives influences of underground currents beneath the house.

Using Belizal's spectrum, I found the color of the vibrations in the magnetic phase to be blue.

Usually, in the process of purifying the energies of a house or office, the color of the vibration at its beginning will be in an electrical phase (negative effect). It will become magnetic (positive effect) only following mental intervention for blocking the energy of the currents. This result merely confirmed the findings of the above measurements: the area was free of underground currents. The entire examination showed the percentage of negative energies arising from underground currents beneath the kibbutz, to be zero.

I drew a deep breath. All values inter-matched and the numbers spoke for themselves! Was it possible that Nir David had no underground currents that cause health problems? This conclusion seemed to fly in the face of logic! There are underground currents everywhere, over the entire face of the globe, even under deserts. There must be another explanation: the underground currents were there, but their negative influence must have been neutralized by other forces operating there.

Continuing to investigate the site, I looked for cosmo-telluric chimneys. An aerial photograph showed that there were some. All the chimneys in Nir David are positive—highly positive, in fact.

FIG. 35:

AERIAL VIEW OF NIR DAVID

The aerial photographs revealed another interesting fact: The position of the chimneys on the map created a triangle. The ratio of the sides called to mind something that I had encountered when studying "regulated lines" with Stéphane Cardinaux. I recalled the triangles we had studied in the course. We had compared their measurements and ratios to those found in renowned ancient paintings, in order to understand what makes them so aesthetic.

So while looking at the layout of the three chimneys in Nir David, I started measuring—on paper—the distances among various points. Then, I took the ratio of the dimensions and compared them to the values we had studied in the course. Those values yielded musical ratios.

To understand what musical ratios are, take a guitar and pluck one of the strings. Then depress a point in the center of the string and pluck once more. The ratio between the two lengths is 2 and the note interval is one octave. Most man-made sacred art works were based on a series of square roots or on the golden ratio (1.618); others, however, were based on a series of musical ratios. The use of musical ratios in architecture was intended to create as many notes as possible while using a minimum of lines in the structure.

The ratios of the triangle at Nir David correlate with the values for the notes *Re, Fa* and *Sol.*

With these amazing results in hand, I was about to set off for Nir David, accompanied by my friend Géèma. We were to meet with my student Yael Berkovitz at her clinic. Minutes before leaving the house, I felt a need, undoubtedly at the prompting of the "Family," to reexamine the aerial photograph I had been working on. Focusing closely on the photograph, I detected a vortex. The etheric manifestation of a vortex is two linked spirals. Spirals always operate in pairs, transmitting energy from one point to the other via the energetic link between them. And at Nir David I found that both spirals of the vortex were located on the lawn. I also examined the mid-point between the three chimneys without taking any measurement. Following my visit to the kibbutz, I discovered that the midpoint was itself a chimney with an extremely high energy level of 4.5 million Bovis. Yael, Géèma and I located, measured and photographed the chimney emplacements. I found that the fourth chimney, the one at the center of the three chimneys, was a hub point for the energy from all three. I put a question to it: "Was it," I asked, "linked with any other site?" The answer was that it was indeed linked—to Kursi, near Lake Kinneret.

The high energy level in Nir David, created by the chimneys and vortices, is evidently strong enough to counteract any negative influence of underground currents or faults. The location of certain buildings and homes above or adjacent to energetic links of the chimneys and of the vortex, explains the longevity of the kibbutz members.

The average energy level in houses positioned on the southern side of the Amal river (commonly known as the Asi), that transverses the kibbutz is about 35,000 Bovis, a very high level for a home. For houses positioned north of the river, the average energy level is 25,000 Bovis. In both cases the energy level is quite high.

My friend Géèma held a channeling session with his source so as to understand the significance and importance of the site. And this is what he was told:

> *A glance at the aerial photograph of Kibbutz Nir David will show*
> *that this is a magical site, since it is symbolized by the sign of infinity.*
> *When the dots are connected, the sign can be clearly seen.*

When the configuration comes to resemble a perfect infinity sign (∞), this place will reach a state of perfection. In the present situation, those living on the kibbutz enjoy high life expectancy, but do not always live in good health. When the[1] symbol attains perfection due to the energies coming into balance, the inhabitants will attain old age in full health with a total halt of the aging process. You will have reached a level at which you will no longer grow old.

Now, it is necessary to make the connection with a neighboring site: Kursi. Kursi has an energy link with Nir David and your friends the Lemurians are doing all they can to assist you.

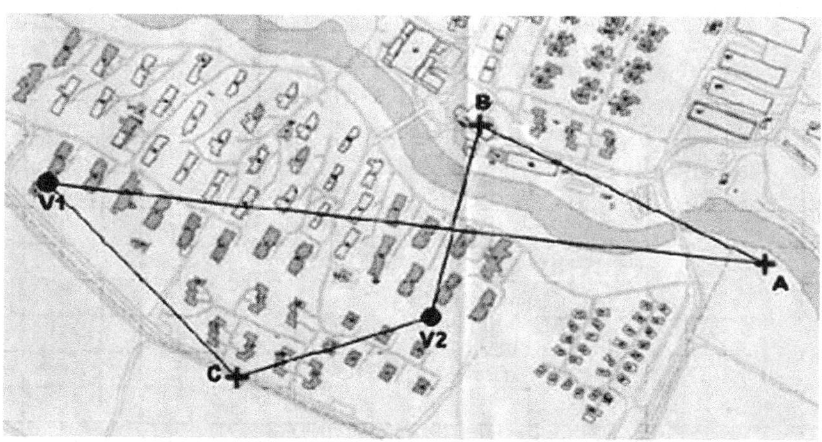

FIG. 36: INFINITY SYMBOL OVER NIR DAVID

On the strength of this message, I mentally activated the link between Nir David and Kursi in July 2008. The connection between them now stands at an energy level of 1.1 million Bovis (up from the original 500,000 Bovis). The energy level at the midpoint of the three chimneys (which, it will be recalled, originally stood at 4.5 million Bovis) has risen to 9 million Bovis. This level is slightly higher than the one measured at Kursi (8 million Bovis).

---

1. Infinity —R.B.

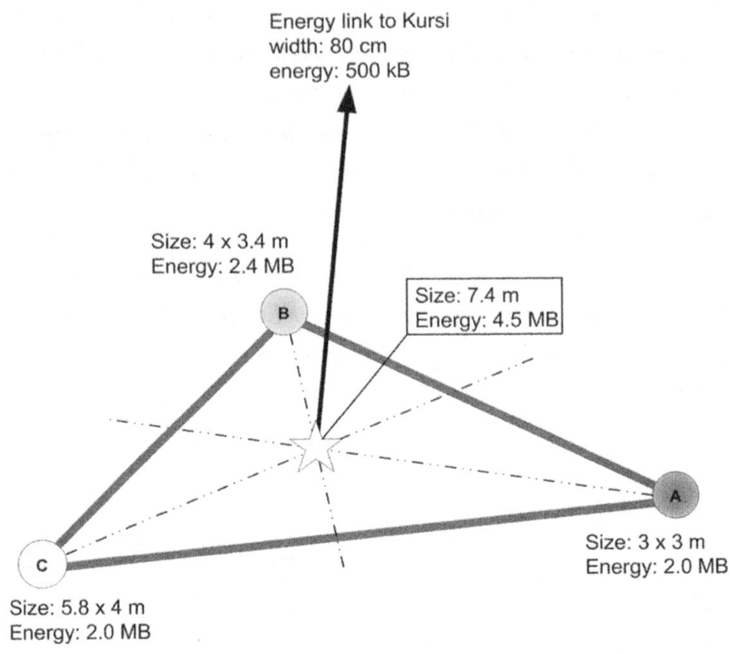

FIG. 37: CHIMNEY DEPLOYMENT AT NIR DAVID

13... Géèma's Home

While we were searching for the 18 sites in Israel, I kept the promise I had made to improve the energies in Géèma's home, in Caesarea. The job took about two hours and the energy level rose from 9,000 Bovis to 58,000 Bovis.[1] This is a normal result for a home after I have finished working on it. Apart from four underground currents (which lower the energy level), I also discovered a cosmo-telluric chimney, which likewise drags down the place's energy level. This chimney, which was very negative (-150,000 Bovis), was located, luckily enough, in an unoccupied room.

I finished what I had to do and as I was taking leave of my friend, he pointed to a palm tree in the garden: "More than 30 plants are growing on that tree," he

---

1. 14,000 Bovis units, you will recall, is the value at a neutral point.

said. This piqued my curiosity. I had seen the tree before, but paid no attention to it. I assumed this was a unique point in terms of energy. I approached the tree with the rods to pinpoint energies. They reacted immediately. Then, I measured the energy level: 220,000 Bovis! The palm tree, I discovered, was situated precisely over a vortex (a positive energy spiral that is connected to another, negative spiral, by means of an energy link). The direction in which the link pointed was a hint that the negative spiral was located outside the property, on an empty lot.

FIG. 38: THE TREE CENTERED IN THE VORTEX, FROM THREE ANGLES

Two days later, Géèma called to tell me that another palm tree, on the other side of the garden, was likewise occupied by a vortex. I went back there to carry out some more measures. Sure enough, there was a vortex there with a positive spiral (220,000 Bovis). This tree, too, was covered to bursting point with a second and even a third generation of vegetation. My experience has taught me that things tend to come in threes; so I went looking for another link that would connect the first tree to a third point. Sure enough, I discovered it—a small, sickly looking plant that had scarcely managed to germinate.

Actually, the spiral at this point was negative (-180,000 Bovis). By means of mental intervention, I caused the two spirals to exchange places with one another, and obtained a positive energy level of 200,000 Bovis.

The idea was that the spirals had been awaiting my coming, having been configured in this manner so as not to operate as a system. This is the same as having a battery inserted backwards so that a radio will not work. By causing them to switch places, I was then able to activate the system. Now the garden had three positive spirals, all interconnected. The energy link between each spiral and the next measured 160,000 Bovis.

Drawing on my experience at Nir David, I began a search, inside the house, for the midpoint between the three spirals. At such a midpoint, the energy level measured very high. I mentally activated the midpoint so as to obtain over a million Bovis!

FIG. 39: PALM TREE AT THE FRONT OF THE HOUSE

The tree nearest the house had surpassed the 1.4 million Bovis point and the diameter of its spiral was now 8.5 meters.[1] The height of the spiral reached 72 meters[2] and its depth 60 meters.[3]

----

1. 28 ft.
2. 236 ft.

At the location of the small plant, there was now an energy level of 1.3 million Bovis. The diameter of the spiral was 9.1 meters,[1] its height 72 meters[2] and its depth 55 meters.[3]

The tree in front of the house also benefited from the change. The energy level around the tree stood at 1.3 million Bovis. The diameter of the spiral was 10.5 meters,[4] its height 72 meters[5] and its depth 55 meters.[6]

In a measurement taken at the center of the house, the level had risen to 1.4 million Bovis, and the diameter was 5.3 meters.[7] The height of the chimney at this location was 150 meters[8] and its depth 115 meters.[9]

FIG. 40: NEGATIVE POINT, AT THE REAR OF THE PROPERTY

I decided to examine the house every three days. The measurements I took were awe-inspiring and amazing: it was like watching a lump of dough treated with yeast that never stops rising. In an effort to understand what was going on, I performed an evaluation of the house from the standpoint of the type of world it stood in. World types are energy fields that correspond to our various auric planes—the physical, etheric, astral, mental, causative, spiritual, pure and divine.

3. 197 ft.
1. 30 ft.
2. 236 ft.
3. 180 ft.
4. 34 ft. 5 in.
5. 236 ft.
6. 337 ft.
7. 17 ft. 3 in.
8. 164 yds.
9. 126 yds.

Three months previously (in May), the house was classed at the level of the physical world.

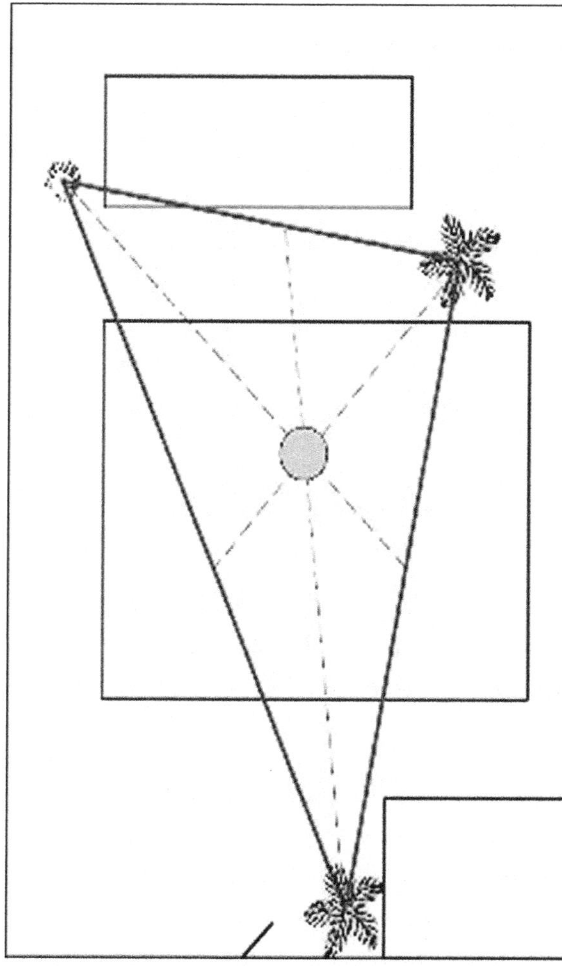

FIG. 41: MAP OF HOUSE, GARDEN AND LOCATION OF TREES AT GÉÈMA'S HOUSE.

On the day on which I activated the three spirals, the level rose to that of the etheric world.

At the time of the current measurement, the house was at the level of the divine world; a level characteristic of major cathedrals.

In terms of energy, the entire lot was vibrating at 280,000 Bovis, an astounding level for a private home. The inside of the house likewise became very energetic reaching a level of 340,000 Bovis. At the midpoint of the three chimneys, in the salon, I measured 11 million Bovis!

The vibration-color of the location changed within three months from orange (negative) to white (the most positive color).

I sensed that this was a high-energy site that might well be one of the 18 sites I had to find. One morning, I came there intending to carry out an idea that had been exercising my mind for two whole days. I stood at the midpoint and, speaking out loud in the ancient Hathor language (that had been in existence for more than 100,000 years), I spoke the words that represent the four elements (water, air, earth and fire). As I spoke, I sensed energies the like of which I had never known. Géèma who was sitting nearby, told me his heart was pounding strongly.

Géèma called upon the "Family" for an explanation as to what was happening with the energy in his home. We were both very excited. I sat beside him expectantly, and the response was not long in coming:

> *What has surfaced in your home exists for more than 20 years. Wherever you go, wherever you are present, you will sense the existence of such an etheric structure. From the moment it was activated — it started to rise gradually until the full realization of its potential. When you noticed this, you were anxious about having to live and sleep with such high energies; but in fact, you know us for ever and you feel absolutely secure in our presence.*
>
> *The day the house became yours (in 1998), we reinforced the young vortices that we had planted there: two positive and one negative. They remained dormant until the day the need transpired for making use of this place.*
>
> *All the changes you have witnessed have made this place a holy site, a point of encounter from which plans for the development of the universe are conducted.*
>
> *In 1998–1999, we installed two very low-intensity positive-energy sources, linked to a negative source. This combination operates at a low level by means of neutralization[1] so that it[2] should not disturb the human and animal kingdoms. On the other hand, we could not prevent the vegetable kingdom from enjoying it, and that explains the density of the vegetation in the garden on the south-eastern side of the house.*
>
> *Even though Yohanna performed an energy cleansing of your house, he could not have noticed this because it[3] was concealed, and we had to send you a signal to initiate its discovery. That is when the true*

---

1. Being maintained in a state of dormancy. —R.B.
2. The vortex.—R.B.
3. A reference to the vortex, the high energy point. —R.B.

work of transformation began. Within exactly seven days, we created a temple with a landing channel at its center.

To this temple[1] a co-creation with you, delegations arrive from three different galaxies, in charge of maintaining the equilibrium of the universe as a whole. They arrive via the central channel. After their arrival, committees disperse in accordance with the topics, in three wings of the temple, in order to hold discussions, to conduct negotiations and to arrive at a common stand. They meet again around the central channel, so as to correct the balance in the universal order. Some of them depart, and the three vortices serve as take-off platforms for various destinations.

The use of this temple allows various delegations to teleport to other regions, to other countries, for the purpose of co-creation with those who are doing the same work as you; after all, you are not the only ones. We regard all of you as an avant-garde battalion, acting for unity, to change human consciousness, to spread peace and brotherhood. All galaxies seek this and the entire universe benefits from it.

Your home has become a temple and great work is in progress. You are seeing its results. Chaos, uncertainty and crises are landing upon wealthy nations. This is a small act of cleansing. You are currently working on the great cleansing to come. The three key words for the future are truth, honesty and integrity. Equipped with these qualities, look upon what is happening—the chaos from within, from which a new order will emerge.

---

1. From here on, the channeling session refers to the house Géèma lives in as a temple.—R.B.

14... Alma

On a hot summer's day in 2008, my friend Géèma and I drove to visit Moshav Alma. The streets were deserted, with not so much as a dog roaming around outside. We were looking for someone who might be familiar with the topography of the place according to an aerial photograph on which I had marked three chimneys. Ultimately, we found a local resident and showed him the photograph. Seemingly at a loss, he scratched his head and said he thought the entire demarcated area was closed and fenced off. Miraculously, however, the gate, on that day, was open.

We found the first chimney at the limit of a pear orchard, the second between two patches of vineyard and the third behind an inaccessible gate. Here we found the chimneys were deeper than they were high.

FIG. 42:
MAP OF ALMA,
NORTH OF SAFED

That evening, as we relaxed on the verandah of the guest house we had rented for the night, Géèma began writing down a message from his "Family."

This site is intended to bring balance and relaxation to hyperactive and absent-minded people; a stay at this site heals past traumas; the healing may take place through the isolation of certain points in the etheric body. A hyperactive individual is one who has been uprooted, who has lost all connection with the earth; as distinct from apathetic people, who have lost all connection with the heavens.

The site maintains the balance of the Upper Galilee region. This site must absolutely and unreservedly not be connected with any other site, because that will create an imbalance. A day will arrive when such connections may be made. As you have discovered, the chimneys are relatively large. For the time being, they are independent and must evolve at their own pace. You also saw that the energy levels are very high. This is possible only because the vegetable kingdom is able to withstand such energies. They are transmitted to people through the consumption of the fruits growing in this region; these are high-energy fruits.

These energies exert a positive influence on the eyes and especially on the optic nerve. Being present on one of these chimneys for a few minutes can, and should, assist in the revival of the elements of the human and animal eye. The consumption of the fruits of the region will also exert a positive influence. You will be able to see for yourselves an improvement in the acuity of your eyesight over time, since you were there long enough to analyze and activate chimneys to a superior level. You also noticed the energy flow among the chimneys. The movement among the chimneys takes place in all directions—both circularly and diagonally—simultaneously.

For example: sometimes the energy moves at an established frequency from the center of the triangle created by the three chimneys from one point to another in a clockwise direction and at other times in an counterclockwise direction. In the resting period, each chimney is charged by means of an internal link among the three chimneys via the central point, which sets off recharging, a rest period and so forth. These energies have an important effect on the glands in general and on the thymus in particular, which boosts the body's immunity. As you continued working on the fenced-off chimney, we intervened so as to assist you. We also sent people to meet you, so as to inform them of what you are doing and stimulate the interest of the inhabitants of the region. We congratulate you on the work you are doing and will support you in whatever difficulties you encounter. We can tell you that the effect will soon be felt, even if many do not understand why; but we and you both know, and all is in accordance with the universal order.

Once more, be blessed. We surround you with light.

Your Family."

During our visit there we selected a few pears in the orchard where the first chimney was located. The fruits were especially large compared to those we found in a more remote locations energy level of the "ordinary" pears was 30,000 Bovis, while that of the "high-energy" pears was 80,000.

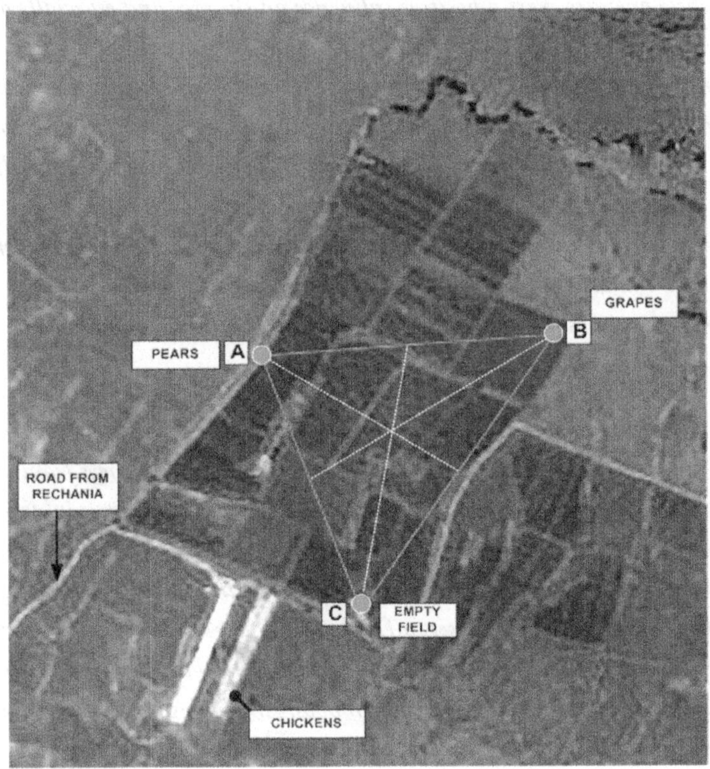

FIG. 43: PRIMARY DETECTION OF ENERGY LOCATIONS

15... Mt. Tabor on the Red Line

It was from one of my students that I first heard of the existence of a special energy line crossing the State of Israel. Then, reports started coming in from other sources, too. This line evidently runs from the Gaza Strip, going up and reaching as far as Damascus and continuing from there to make its way around the world. The first time I worked on the line was in 2005. At around that time, the second Lebanese war was taking place and the line was extremely negative. After working on the line, its energy level rose, fell and rose again. I resumed work on the line in June 2008. By recharging the energy line I was able to raise its energy level to 11 million Bovis. This line is very important for Israel and for the region as a whole, since it raises the frequency over the entire country.

Mount Tabor is located in Lower Galilee, 17 km west of the Sea of Galilee (Lake Kinneret), at an elevation of 562 m. The mountain's importance stems from its strategic control of the junction of the Galilee's north-south route with the east-west road of the Jezreel Valley. In 1101, under the control of the Crusaders, the Benedictine monks rebuilt a ruined basilica and erected a fortified abbey.

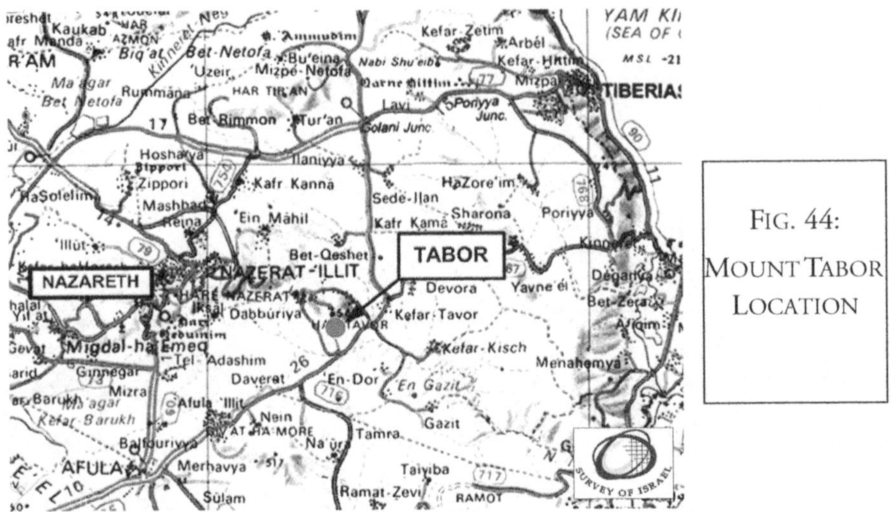

Fig. 44: Mount Tabor Location

On the north-western side of the church is a cave named after Melchizedek, King of Shalem. According to Christian tradition, it was here that the meeting took place between Abraham and the King of Shalem.

On Mt. Tabor, Barak son of Avinoam gathered "ten thousand men of the children of Naphtali and of the children of Zebulun" to fight the army of Sisera the Canaanite, as narrated in the Book of Judges. Sisera, who was the commander of King Jabin's army, was defeated and destroyed by Barak in the Jezreel Valley.

The Christians believe this was where Jesus underwent his Transfiguration and began to radiate all around him and was seen conversing with Moses and Elijah.

Calling to mind the significance of the mountain as a point on the red line, I also wanted to check out the possibility that Mt. Tabor is one of the 18 sites that it was my job to find. Using aerial photographs, I focused on locating the various singularities of Mt. Tabor. I immediately found the high-energy line passing dead center between the two buildings on the hill, the church and the monastery. I discovered something I had not known before I started searching, namely that there is a link between the points of the high energy sites in Israel and the red line, the energy line that passes through the entire State of Israel.

FIG. 45:
THE ENERGY
LINE THAT
CROSSES
MOUNT
TABOR

The line discovered on Mt. Tabor passes between and not over buildings. The high energy of the line is too great for human beings, for continuous exposure. This may explain the extraordinary circumstances of the means of access to Mt. Tabor. The way the daily swarms of tourists visiting the church on the mountaintop are handled is sometimes so strange, as to be ridiculous. At the foot of the mountain lie a number of villages populated by Bedouins who settled there at the instigation of the government of Israel, when the State was commemorated in 1948. To assure them of employment and a livelihood (thereby avoiding trouble), they were given exclusivity in transporting visitors to the church on the mountaintop, by means of minibuses operated by bad-tempered drivers. One may arrive at a plaza where a large signpost proclaims "Tabor Terminal," and sure enough, visitors may often undergo a fairly dangerous up-and-down "flight" negotiating hairpin bends. Imagine several bus loads of pilgrims reaching the terminal square on a daily basis, to be met, of course, by retail stores and a buffet for the travelers' convenience, during the long wait for the next minibus.

Indeed, the spectacle makes one wonder about the quality of life in proximity to so powerful an energy line.

In July 2008, Géèma and I drove up Mt. Tabor in a private car. I had previously identified four chimneys and one vortex. There was no possible access to the location at which the negative spiral of the vortex and one of the chimneys were situated. I mentally activated the chimneys that were accessible, increasing their diameter, their energy level and their elevation/depth.

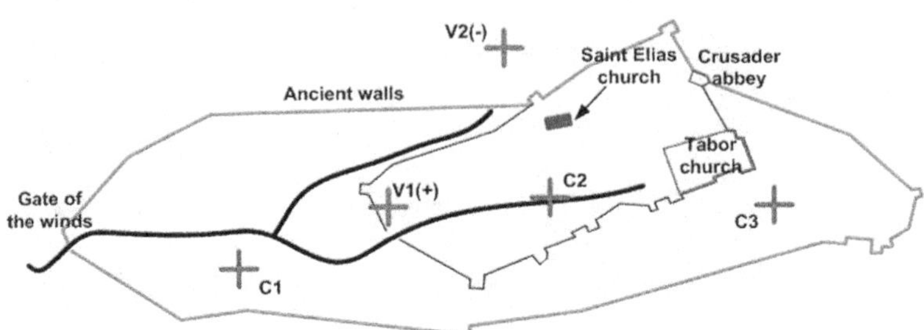

FIG. 46: LOCATION OF SINGULARITIES

Géèma held a channeling session while we were there and the following was what emerged:

The Mt. Tabor region is very important as far as your work is concerned. An artery passes through this site and is linked to certain organs of the terrestrial globe. This energy line does not detract from the importance of the vortex and the chimneys, since they are also linked to the great artery you have identified. Many people ask you why you are doing this work. Know that in each of the five Afro-Asian regions there are people who are involved just as you are and we coordinate all of your activities. You can start seeing results: an interlude of calm with your Palestinian neighbors, prospects for talks in all areas and recently with Syria. From an internal aspect the great opportunity has arrived, and will pay off before the end of the year. There will be a number of upheavals, but order will be maintained. Mt. Tabor is exceedingly rich in vortices and chimneys; so far, you have not found them all. The energies located on Tabor have a beneficial effect on people suffering from anorexia or those who suffer from compulsive disorders and various addictions. For those in need, we recommend a stay in this area.

16... Megiddo

During this time, Géèma and I had made a habit of touring the length and breadth of the country on Saturdays, following the promptings of our intuition and seeking the missing energy sites in a system. These excursions, invariably winding up at this or that fish restaurant, were now enhanced by the pleasant company of a new lady friend by the name of Sophie.

One Saturday, we were planning a trip to Kibbutz Ginosar, where you could sail Lake Kinneret in a glass-bottomed boat and gaze into the watery depths. That morning, Géèma called to announce a change of plan. The boat-trips, he had heard on the news, had been cancelled due to a storm over Lake Kinneret, so he suggested we go to Megiddo instead. I had never been to Megiddo, so Sophie and I took off and met Géèma there.

When Megiddo proved to be one of the 18 sites, we joked, my friends and I, that the "Family" had organized the storm on Lake Kinneret so that we shouldn't go to the wrong place by mistake!

Megiddo is located not far from Nazareth and Yokne'am, south of Haifa, at the foot of a mountain pass facing the west of the Jezreel Valley. At the very first measurement, we discovered the fact that the Megiddo site was vital to our mission. It had an energy level of 9 million Bovis!

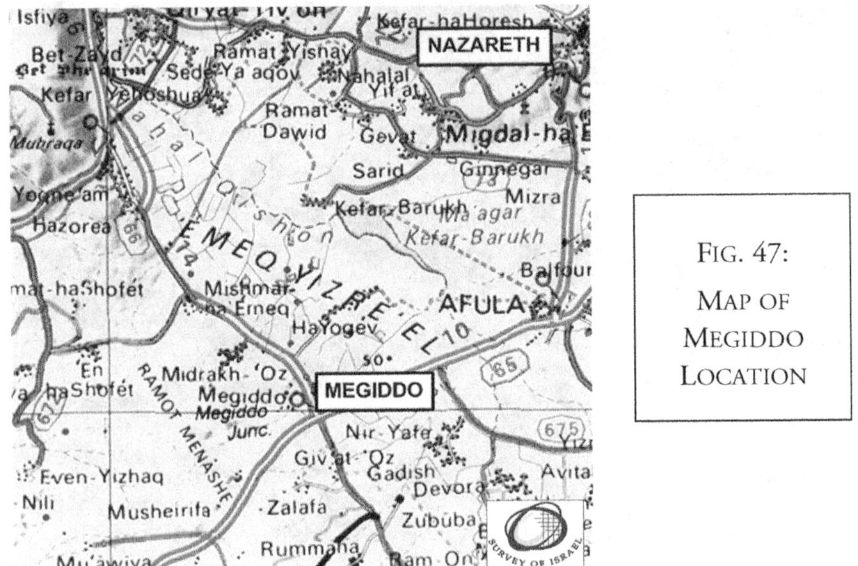

FIG. 47: MAP OF MEGIDDO LOCATION

This is an interesting place, historically speaking. Tel Megiddo is positioned strategically as a fortress town rising above the road between Egypt and Syria. The town has been through more than 20 different historical periods and is today one of the sites worth visiting, thanks to King Solomon's stables and the ancient aqueduct quarried into the rock. The Tel consists of 30 superimposed strata, the "oldest" aged more than 7,000 years, while the "youngest" dates from the year 400 CE.

The New Testament refers to this site as Armageddon and it is to be the battlefield of the War of the End of Days (the war of Gog and Magog) where the forces of good will battle the forces of evil.

An initial search turned up three chimneys. The first chimney was located next to the entrance to the mountain. Géèma strode ahead of me. When I reached his side, he said: "It's here." I ran a test using antennas, and, sure enough, he was right! I took measurements and then activated the chimney.

A few minutes later, Géèma got a message from the "Family," saying that locating the other two chimneys physically was unnecessary. So I located them on the site map, took measurements and made a note of the results for myself.

As I was busying myself with the measurements, Géèma got another "transmission" from his "Family":

> *This is a message for Yohanna. We owe him an explanation because he is doing a great deal of work. We led you to Megiddo since you almost missed the place; but this is an important annex site. You were able to measure its power. The energy level of this site varies and it is linked to Mt. Tabor; it ensures regulation of the Gaza – Damascus line, via Mt. Tabor. These variations enable this energy artery to be activated.*

> *For example: when the artery is operating at a constant rate, Megiddo does not intervene, but when the pace slows and the energy declines, a request is generated for a flow of energy; and Megiddo compensates for this drop and supplies the line with the necessary energy. In the reverse instance, Megiddo will absorb the surplus. This is the reason why the activation of one chimney suffices in order to activate the other two. Our joint work means that we see what is concealed from you. On the other hand, you are doing what we cannot do.*

> *We brought you to the center of the chimney. Yohanna was incredulous: he believes in his antennas. At a certain moment, he took a measurement that gave the overall value of the site, following activation. We announced 25 million and he found 26 million. This is the effect of the strong wind that is blowing today. The true result is 25 million and you should have corrected it; you did not do so because you have doubt in yourself. Have faith!*

> *Since we are speaking of auxiliary sites, we would note the Kursi is one of them. But Kursi[1] is an annex of a number of sites and it polarizes/ nourishes them when necessary.*

> *We bless you.*

> *Your Family.*

---

1. Unlike Megiddo, which is an annex of Mt. Tabor only. —R.B

*N.B.: After what you have done, **the battle of Armageddon will not take place!***

Armed with this information, we started to look for the link with Mt. Tabor. The mountain is visible from a distance. I measured the link between Megiddo and Mt. Tabor. The energy level of Megiddo also rose once the chimneys had been activated. After that, I also activated the link between the two sites.

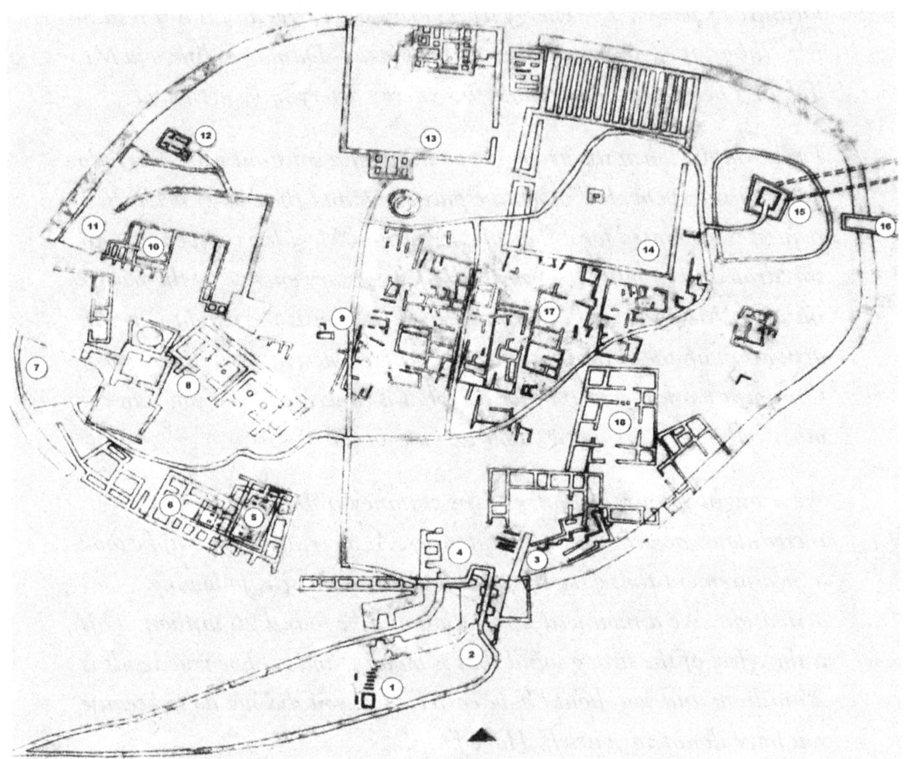

FIG. 48: IDENTIFICATION OF MEGIDDO RUINS

1.	Reservoir	7.	Northern lookout	13.	Southern palace
2.	City gate	8.	Temples	14.	Southern stables
3.	Palace gate	9.	Royal tomb	15.	Water system
4.	City gate	10.	Eastern palace	16.	Gallery
5.	Northern stables	11.	Southern lookout	17.	Assyrian quarter
6.	Northern palace	12.	Houses	18.	Assyrian palaces

17... The Seven Hills

I found the next high-energy site in the middle of nowhere. When looking at a geographical map of Israel, the area in which it is located stands out as being thinly populated. This is an astounding fact, for two reasons: one, since it is at the very center of the country, and two, because in ancient times, this was a populated area, as indicated by the numerous tumuli[1] that are still scattered around. This is the Lachish region, described in the Bible as a place in whose fields a great many battles were fought between the Judeans and the Philistines, an example being the one between David and Goliath

As soon as I had traced the general location on the map, I looked for a nearby community and obtained an aerial photograph of the region. I zoomed in

---

1. Plural of tumulus, a mound of earth and stones raised over a grave or graves.

until I started to see roads. At that time, apart from the starting point on the map, which was marked as Mt. Mendel Gad, near Kibbutz Lachish, I had no idea where the place was.

Using a pendulum, I discovered a number of points surrounding the central point. These points, seven in number, were all positive chimneys. Their energy levels, as remotely measured in millions of Bovis units, were as follows:

Chimney	C1	C2	C3	C4	C5	C6	C7
Bovis, M	2.3	2.1	2.0	2.2	1.9	2.2	2.1

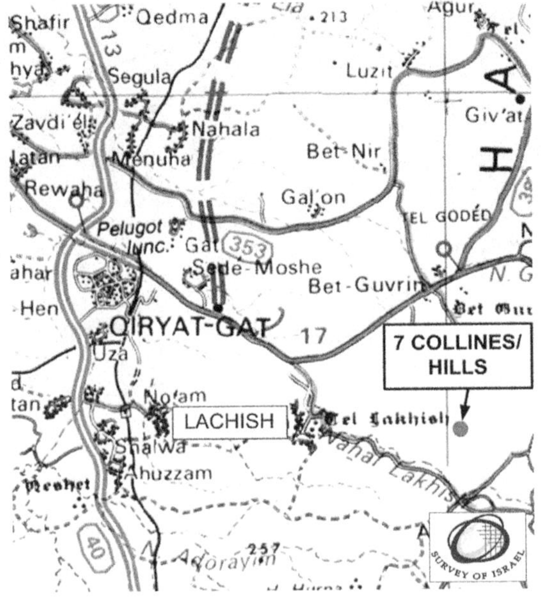

FIG. 49:

GEOGRAPHICAL LOCATION OF SEVEN HILLS

With these promising initial data in hand, I got going. My first trip led me in the general direction of Kiryat Gat and Kibbutz Lachish. Arriving at that area, I followed the sign posting to Mt. Gad, inadvertently passing the location I was headed for. After driving for some time, I came to the conclusion that I was lost. And then it started raining. I was about to give up, when a car drove up beside me. I asked the driver (who turned out to be from Kibbutz Lachish) whether he was familiar with the site in my aerial photograph. He took me there in the pouring rain. There was no doubt in my mind that the "Family" had sent him to me.

All I could do, considering the weather, was to stay in the car and look at the muddy field and the adjoining hills. Taking an energy measurement from where I was parked, I got 2 million Bovis, similar to my remotely taken measurements—an energy level that is equivalent to that usually found in cathedrals. I decided to come back another day. On my way back, I took some shots of various landmarks that would help me locate the place in the future.

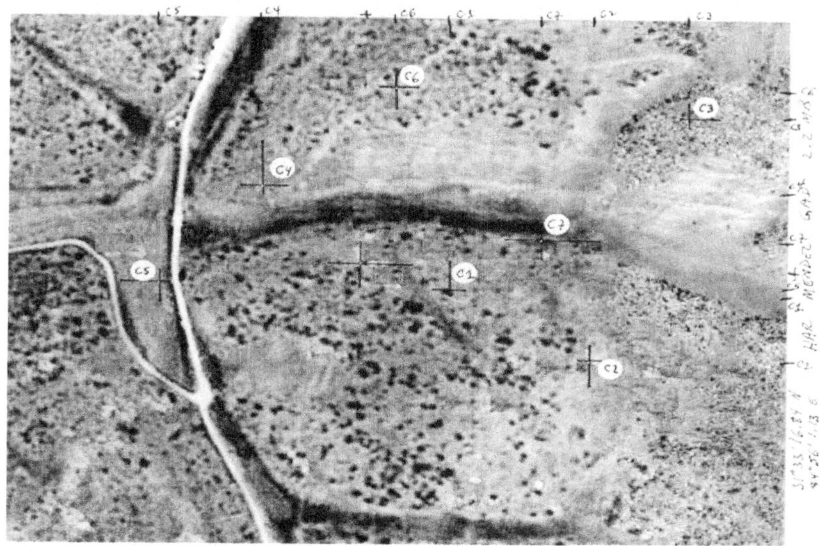

FIG. 50: CHIMNEY LOCATIONS, SEVEN HILLS

Next time, I returned to this site with Géèma. Because we found no name on the map for the specific area we had reached, I called it the "Seven Hills," to reflect its geographical configuration.

We went in search of the chimneys in accordance with the research I had conducted with the aid of the aerial photograph. Starting with the chimney nearest the road (chimney C5), we activated chimneys C4 and C6.

While I was activating chimney C6, Géèma got a message from the "Family" saying that there was no need to locate and activate all the seven chimneys. The minute we activated chimney C2, all the others would be activated too. What a relief! This meant less work for us to do under the blazing sun. We proceeded to activate chimney C2 and with that the job was completed.

At first, all the chimneys seemed to be the same color (white). Later we discovered that each chimney had a different color. After activation, I found that all values had distinctly increased, to the point of doubling in size.

Once we had completed the measurements, we left the area and parked under a tree. Géèma began a channeling session with "the Family":

You are this day at the bottom of the valley of the Seven Hills, an old, very old crater of a dormant volcano. The earth crust at this location is less than 4 km; you can imagine the natural advantages this region can have on the geothermal aspect.

Seven hills, seven chimneys...... why this number? Each one of the chimneys has one of the colors of a rainbow. We cannot tell you the beauty of this site in our dimension! And in combining the seven colors we obtain white, the color you measured at each chimney.

Each one of the seven chimneys is connected via a ray originating from a planet.[1] It will be easy for you to find out which ray comes from which planet. The seven rays when united form a big white ray connected to Sirius.

Of all of the sites discovered until now, this one is of capital importance, since it is the source of all these healing energies that you have discovered or that you will discover.

This day, you yourselves have dwelled in these energies and you will benefits from their effects.

The day will come when we shall explain how to connect to other sites already found or to be found. This site is a central site and is connected to seven other sites.

All this is very complex for you, but trust us and all will be explained and communicated in due time.

Back home, I got busy learning about Sirius. I found that it was also called the Alpha Star, of the Canis Majoris constellation (the Greater Dog). This is the brightest star in the Greater Dog group that denotes Orion's hunting dog, and it is therefore usually called the Dog Star. Because of its brilliance, Sirius is the champion of all twinklers, the effect caused by variable refraction in the Earth's atmosphere. The star is a white hydrogen-fusing dwarf with a temperature of 10,153° Celsius. It is bright in part because it is indeed rather luminous, 26 times more so than the Sun, but mostly because it is nearby. It is

---

1. One of the seven principal planets in our solar system. —R.B.

a mere 8.6 light years away, just double that of the closest star to the Earth (Alpha Centauri) and the fifth closest star system. According to ancient mystic theories common to several civilizations, humans have a very great affinity for Sirius.

I was curious about the seven chimneys and wished to find the colors unique to each chimney and the planet to which it belongs, as described to us in the channeling session. I did this with the aid of the pendulum.

Color	Planet	Chimney
Yellow	Saturn	C1
Orange	Jupiter	C2
Indigo	Neptune	C3
Green	Venus	C4
Red	Uranus	C5
Blue	Mercury	C6
Violet	Mars	C7

After that, I drew the links interconnecting the chimneys.

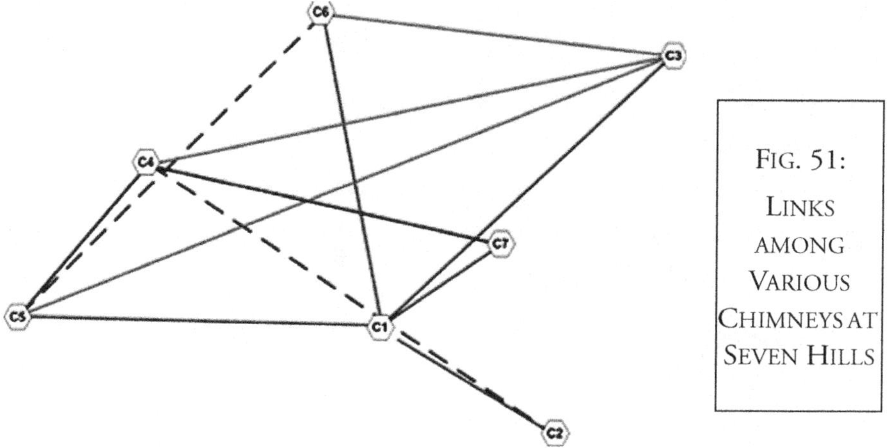

FIG. 51:

LINKS AMONG VARIOUS CHIMNEYS AT SEVEN HILLS

In December, I took a third trip to the "Seven Hills," this time with my friend Sophie. I hadn't the slightest notion why I had to get back there, but I knew, I would be guided as to what to do. When we arrived, I examined some of the links among the chimneys and measured the energy levels.

I felt there must be another reason as to why I drove an hour and a half to reach this location. I looked again at the aerial view and checked out the central cross, the one that was unmarked. With the pendulum, I asked if this was the link to Sirius, as told in the channeling session. "Yes" is what I got for an answer. I started to walk toward the location indicated on the map.

Sophie was following me, a few meters behind. All of the sudden I heard: Look at the "door."

"What 'door'?"

"This door," she said, pointing to a tree.

Sophie is of Russian extraction, but her Hebrew is certainly good enough to be able to differentiate a tree from a door. Then it occurred to me that the tree may as well be a door—the Doorway to Sirius. At the tree, I found a chimney of large proportions. It had an energy level of 19 million Bovis.

Fig. 52:
The "Door" to Sirius

It was a wonderful discovery!

The tree stood out conspicuously in its surroundings, which consisted mostly of low brushwood, a few bushes and lots of herbage. It was growing between gigantic stones, as if from out of the very rock. After a while, as I grasped one of the branches of the tree, I started spontaneously uttering words in the ancient language that I always use in the harmonization ceremony: words in the language of the Hathors. Like a mantra they came spilling out from me, again and again. Once I had stopped, I measured the energy level again. The energy had surprisingly risen to 25 million Bovis. To complete the job, I mentally activated the chimney. After that, the values increased even more. It was a confirmation; I understood why I had felt the urge to come to the Seven Hills that day: to find the Doorway to Sirius.

That spring, we returned, Sophie and I, to the Seven Hills. On the way, we stopped at the Kibbutz Lachish. We parked at the entrance to the kibbutz. Measuring the general energy level of the kibbutz, I found an astonishing level of 80,000 Bovis! A similar measurement three months earlier had shown a value of 50,000 Bovis. The activation of the 18 sites had evidently contributed to the astounding rise of energy in the area. After all, the kibbutz is located only a few kilometers from the Seven Hills.

There was a gradual increase in energy levels as we drew closer to the site. Sophie and I approached the tree and sat down in its shade. There were millions of flies there. Were they, perhaps, being drawn by the special energies of the place? In examining the area of the tree I measured an energy level of 280 million Bovis! What powerful activity!

After a short prayer whose purpose was to enhance the surrounding harmony, the result achieved was 320 million Bovis; a few words uttered by me raised it by 40 million Bovis!

Unbelievable!

We stayed a few minutes longer to meditate before returning to the car, leaving the flies to their own devices.

On the way back, we passed for a second time a herd of cows grazing in the meadow, and my friend asked me to stop so she could take a few photographs. Suddenly, she was pointing excitedly. I couldn't believe my eyes. A cow that was approaching us at a run had her back tattooed with the number 320; just like the result of the last measurement I had taken at the Doorway to Sirius: 320 million Bovis. It may seem strange, but I sometimes regard events such as these as a sign from "the Family," a little wink meant to confirm that the value I had measured was indeed accurate.

FIG. 53:

A HINT FROM THE FAMILY

18... Seven Hills Auxiliary Sites

It took a great deal of time and effort on my part to identify the seven other sites located around the Seven Hills. I performed all this work remotely, including the activation of the sites. This was because, apart from the geographical distance that lay between me and certain places, there was also the fact that some were located in the Palestinian territories.

Given that each chimney in the Seven Hills sites is linked to another site, I sought connective routes on the aerial photograph. The pendulum gave me seven points on the circumference of the page. After that, I had to find out which point was appropriate for each chimney. Certain lines intersect without difficulty. They are of different colors and therefore of different frequency. To some extent, it's like optical fibers that carry different signals, each at a different frequency, without interfering with one another. This table provides the final location of the seven auxiliary sites:

Link	Near	Longitude	Latitude	Site Energy	Link Energy
C1	Rahat	34°47'E	26° 31'N	5	140
C2	Soussia	6°35'E	23° 31'N	2.4	170
C3	Halhul/Beit ahil	5°35'E	35° 31'N	3	110
C4	Nachala	49°34'E	40° 31'N	2	120
C5	Snoqeda	32° 34'E	26° 31'N	1.5	100
C6	Beit Shemesh	56° 34'E	45° 31'N	2.5	180
C7	Hebron	13° 35'E	28° 31'N	3	170

Site Energy is in MB, millions of Bovis units.
Link Energy is in kB, thousands of Bovis units.

Once I had the general directions for each site, I extended the lines with my pendulum and sought an intersection. I continued to work, passing the pendulum over the aerial photograph, so as to find the estimated location, and after that, magnifying the location and restarting the search with the aid of the pendulum. In that way, I found each of the seven sites.

THE FINAL CONFIGURATION

Each auxiliary site connects to the Seven Hills by a colored link:

Site	Color
C1	Indigo
C2	Green
C3	Violet
C4	Yellow
C5	Red
C6	Blue
C7	Orange

The next channeling session highlighted the importance of the work at the Seven Hills and its seven linked sites:

Remember the work you did at that enchanting site of the Seven
Hills? Read what you were told one more time, and you will

understand why Yohanna[1] did important work that day. You will be seeing the results very soon. The Seven Hills are linked to seven sites which you will be activating likewise. Each of the sites fulfils an exact function. But you must consider all of them as an organ in its own right. The other sites operate independently, even if they are interlinked. The Seven Hills and the auxiliary sites around it operate like a heart. They are like a bright star and visible from many galaxies. This is an energy generator for those who are approaching Earth. It also allows visitors to adapt their vibrations and harmonize them, prior to landing at the various sites that will be discovered near Mizpe Ramon.

The physical discomfort you are experiencing derives from the acceleration of the activation of vortices on the entire planet. As we have said, people from other countries and continents are taking part in this work. In another seven-eight days, things will stabilize and your body will revert to its normal state, but on another plane. You are now going to find the links among the sites identified.

You will complete your work before the end of the year, and then the second phase will begin, and after that – the third.

May you be blessed!

Your Family.

Three weeks later, we received another communication following my request for information on the auxiliary sites connected to Seven Hills:

The question that is preoccupying Yohanna is: what is the purpose of the seven sites surrounding Seven Hills? At this stage of your work in co-creation, there is not necessarily a specific application for each of the 18 sites. All sites originate from a source. They permit all persons present at any one of the sites to be treated and cured, just by their intention, and not by the specific energy radiating from that location.

---

1. Refers to me, Richard. —R.B.

As we explained on a previous occasion, this major site operates like an organ, and that is how it should be regarded.

The work you did and are doing with the 18 sites is part of a more comprehensive job. You do not have the entire picture of everything that is being done; we do. That is why we are able to guide and help you. When you complete your work, it will be you helping us. It is too soon to explain everything to you. You will gain greater understanding once you evolve in the multi-dimension. Your dimension does not allow you to realize this.

Go on with the work that is still before you, and you will discover a slightly clearer picture of what is being done. From where you are, it is very hard for you to understand the tremendous work you have done. Truly, you have done a marvelous job. Thanks to you, things will improve.

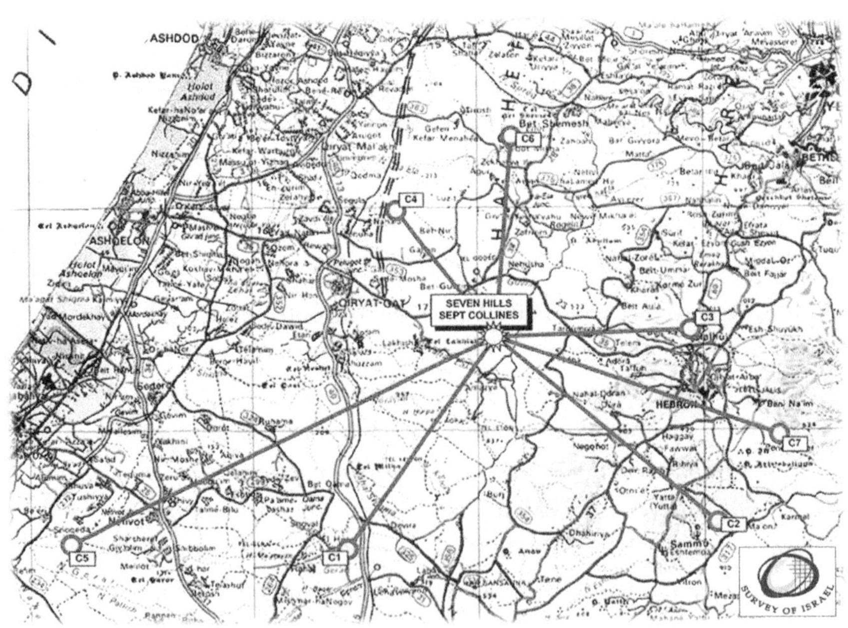

Fig. 54: Final Location of the Seven Hills
and its 7 Auxiliary Sites

19... System Operation

By the end of 2009, I had activated and gradually linked together all the 18 sites. At the initial stage, I connected the sites while visiting Géèma's home. I used a map of Israel showing all the sites, including the cross-Israel high-energy line. Using the pendulum, and referring to each site individually, I inquired whether it was tied to other sites in the vicinity. In accordance with the answers I received, I used different colored threads to highlight the links on the map. Then, I mentally connected the groups of sites. I also asked whether a site was linked to the energy artery. Sometimes, indeed, there was such a link. The map shows how, by means of the links, two (figure-eight) infinity symbols were created. A third shape of this kind came to light later on in the south (and includes Avdat and the two sites in the vicinity of the Mizpe Ramon area).

Indeed, I remembered the channeling given to us on the figure eights:

Now let's talk about the energy-intensive line to which almost all the sites are linked, directly or indirectly. This high energy line is an artery. We already spoke about this when you were on Mt. Tabor. As long as this line is operating at a proper energy level, the situation will remain stable from the point of view of humans. But in the event of any hindrance or slowdown, problems will occur. As you saw, the two signs of infinity failed to reach their ideal form, especially that of the north — it did not attain the perfect figure-eight shape.

You will receive another, third symbol when you complete your work. In the future, you will have to connect all three to this place, so that the energy can flow unimpeded and with no resistance on the part of human consciousness.

Go on with the work that is still before you, and you will discover a slightly clearer picture of what is being done. From the point you are at, it is very hard for you to understand the tremendous work you have done. Truly, you have done a marvelous job. Thanks to you, things will improve.

One can clearly see the star created by Seven Hills and its seven secondary sites. Finally, Megiddo can be seen to be linked with Mt. Tabor alone, conforming to its function as an energy regulator for the artery that passes through Mt. Tabor.

At this point in time, I was still missing two sites. In a channeling session, my friend Géèma drew my attention to the fact that there are two sites that are supposed to complete a circle with Avdat. I promptly got down to a search with the aid of a map and a pendulum. One such site, Bor Chemet, is located just before Makhtesh Ramon, and the other, Mizpe Ha-Meshar, is located after Makhtesh Ramon next to Maaleh Har.

My friend Sophie and I drove to Bor Chemet along the Mizpe Ramon road. The place was not easy to find, but we did reach it after circling around a few times. Walking in front of me, Sophie found the location of the first chimney. An examination proved that she was right. There was a strong wind that day, making it difficult for me to work with the antennas. I began taking measurements. I found a similarity between the operation of the chimneys here and those at Alma. Here, too, it turned out that they link up with one central point. After activating the chimneys, I once more measured the energy level of the site as a whole, and found that it had reached 23 million Bovis.

The second site, Mizpeh Ha-Meshar, is a large, windy plain stretching as far as the line of high mountains that rise in the distance and form its boundary. On the aerial photograph I spotted four chimneys arranged to form a cross. After activating them, I measured the energy level of the entire site again: 26 million Bovis. Back home, I linked Bor Chemet and Mizpe Ha-Meshar to Avdat.

With information on the 18 sites at hand, I activated the entire system with the aid of a map of Israel. The results were most surprising. As I worked, I was feeling full of energy, as if hovering in mid-air. This feeling persisted for several minutes. I asked for the energy to flow everywhere, amongst all the sites and also through the energy artery; then I connected the central point of each infinity symbol, to the other two. For me, this was an absolute tempest of energy; it left me fairly drained.

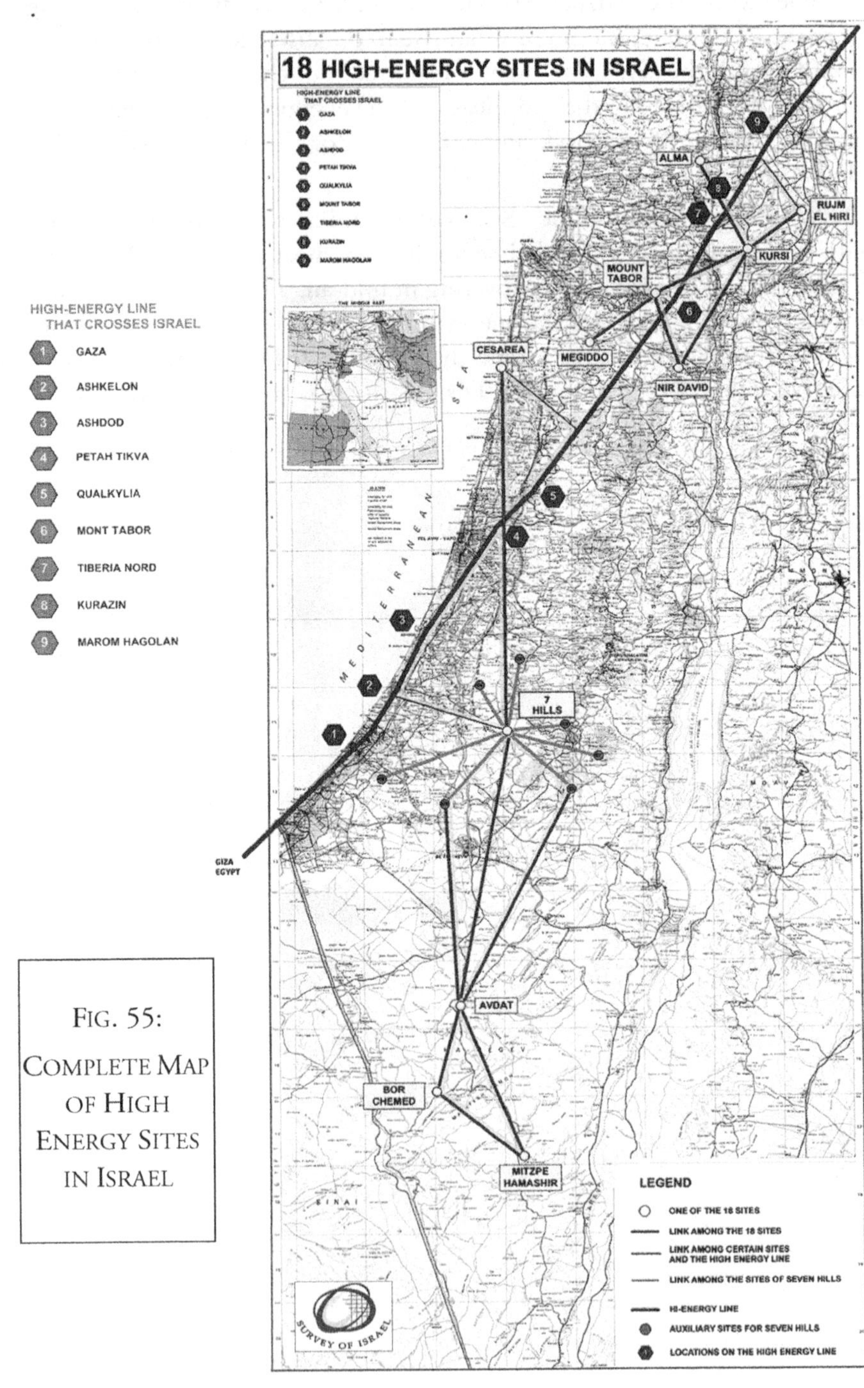

FIG. 55:

COMPLETE MAP OF HIGH ENERGY SITES IN ISRAEL

20... Project Completion

The results of my work became apparent to me over the next few days. After gradually rising, the system energy level stabilized. Measurements showed that the effect of the new energies included all areas of the State of Israel. In the cities of Tel Aviv, Jerusalem, Haifa and Gaza, I instituted a follow-up of the energy levels (the results are provided hereafter).

From Israel I passed to the neighboring countries. There, too, the results were impressive.

Summary table of the follow-up of the energy levels of the high-energy sites in Israel (in millions of Bovis units):

Date:	2009							2010			2011
Location:	4/19	4/26	5/15	5/21	5/31	7/14	9/11	4/9	4/16	8/4	8/11
Energy line	135	170	280	300	320	320	340	470	530	510	1050
Kursi	81	115	160	200	210	230	260	380	480	440	1050
Alma	82	93	140	160	200	200	250	400	500	490	960
Tabor	72	93	140	170	190	210	290	380	450	520	1310
House Caesarea	94	99	120	140	160	230	300	405	480	520	1350
Megiddo	83	90	160	190	190	220	290	390	480	480	1200
Rujm el-Hiri	93	110	200	220	210	250	290	410	530	605	2300
Nir David	80	96	140	160	180	240	300	380	460	510	950
Avdat	84	92	150	190	180	250	300	400	420	460	1200
Mizpe	91	99	150	180	190	230	290	380	430	460	910
Bor Chemet	83	91	130	180	200	220	290	410	410	470	850
Seven Hills	112	118	260	290	300	340	335	490	595	730	1930
C1	86	93	130	160	160	230	300	360	420	420	950
C2	84	91	120	140	150	210	300	350	380	440	850
C3	82	90	120	140	160	220	300	370	370	460	900
C4	82	92	115	135	160	230	300	360	360	430	1200
C5	82	93	130	160	155	220	310	370	370	410	920
C6	83	91	115	140	150	225	300	340	370	420	1100
C7	82	92	110	135	165	220	300	360	360	440	950

Energy in the cities in Israel (in kB, thousands of Bovis units):

Date:	2009							2010		2011
Location:	1/16	4/24	5/8	5/21	6/3	7/14	9/11	4/9	4/16	8/11
Tel Aviv	6	15	17	20	23	28	28	29	29	29
Haifa	3.5	8	13	16	22	26	28	29	29	28
Gaza	2.5	5	8	10	16	24	28	28	28	22
Jerusalem	6	12	14	20	26	27	30	32	32	40

Energy in neighboring countries (in kB, thousands of Bovis units):

Date:	2009		2010		2011
Location:	1/16	9/11	4/9	4/16	8/11
Jordan	9	26	29	29	30
Egypt	13	29	31	31	16
Syria	12	25	30	30	14
Lebanon	8	25	30	30	28
Israel	13	26	34	38	30

On May 10, 2009, when the system had been in operation for almost a month with astonishing results, the "Family" channeled a message to Géèma:

Here you are, in front of this network that has been composed and co-created together with you; without you, we could not have realized it. It is not perfect in your eyes because you still lack the overview of the other systems that are in process of being created. The network will improve over time and will assume its final shape once it is connected; for the present, it is fulfilling its function and acting upon everything, and you are feeling this.

Other networks are in process of being created. To that end, we do not necessarily need the help of people on your planet (this message is addressed specifically to the Son of Isaiah to reassure him, if he does not encounter other individuals like himself).

Once the five networks in your region are completed, they will merge into a single system, and the levels will rise to beyond what you are able to conceive, even if you are accustomed to high energy levels, corresponding to other dimensions and planes. For example: we draw your attention to this site that you designated "Géèma Home"; what energy levels did the vortices have when you discovered them? And what levels are there now? And it isn't over yet.

We will now allow you some time to rest, because you have completed the work with great diligence and we thank you. In another five-six days, the energy levels will stabilize, and that will give rise to several events: healing of planets, of people, of the animal, vegetable and mineral kingdoms, and many others you are not acquainted with; you will see greater tranquillity taking shape amongst pure-hearted humans.

The others will have to cope with mishaps, disruptions and violence, and the cleansing will continue in other forms: wars, meteorological events and earthquakes. You can gaze on all this as calmly as if you were watching a movie; you are not involved! During this period of respite you will have a sense of relief, of lightness, and if by chance you feel a little tired or listless, take the map of the 18 sites and immerse yourselves in its energy. You will feel like new… try it! This is your gift!

May you be blessed.

Your Family

21... The Question of Jerusalem

When I told people about my search for high-energy sites in Israel, many of them, reasonably enough, asked me: "What about Jerusalem?" Jerusalem is deemed to be a holy city, by the three monotheistic religions. For the Jews, this is the site of the Temple Mount, where once the holy Temple stood, and where its last remaining vestige, the Western Wall, is situated. Believers flock to it from all over the world to pray and ask for miracles. The Church of the Holy Sepulcher is an important pilgrimage site for Christians and within a relatively short radius from there are the Stations of the Cross, on the Via Dolorosa, through which Jesus passed en route to his crucifixion. Also, according to Muslim tradition, the holy site from which Mohammed ascended to heaven is on the Temple Mount. It stands to reason that these sites should be highly energetic and in fact they are, but a long history of conflicts and bloodshed, have generated much suffering pain throughout the ages.

Back in March 2001, I was planning to raise the energy in the Old City of Jerusalem with the aid of some of my students, so as to create an atmosphere of peace. Based on John Michell's book *The Temple at Jerusalem—a Revelation*, my idea was to conduct several harmonization ceremonies simultaneously at selected locations in the Old City.

Michell's book has a map showing the layout of the Old City of Jerusalem, over which two pentagrams are superimposed. According to this layout, the gates of the wall are located precisely over the two pentagrams' points. What I had in mind was to station a number of students at each such point, equipping them with tools necessary for the harmonization of Jerusalem. Right about that time, the second Intifada (Palestinian riot) broke out, making East Jerusalem too dangerous a place to enter – and all plans were called off.

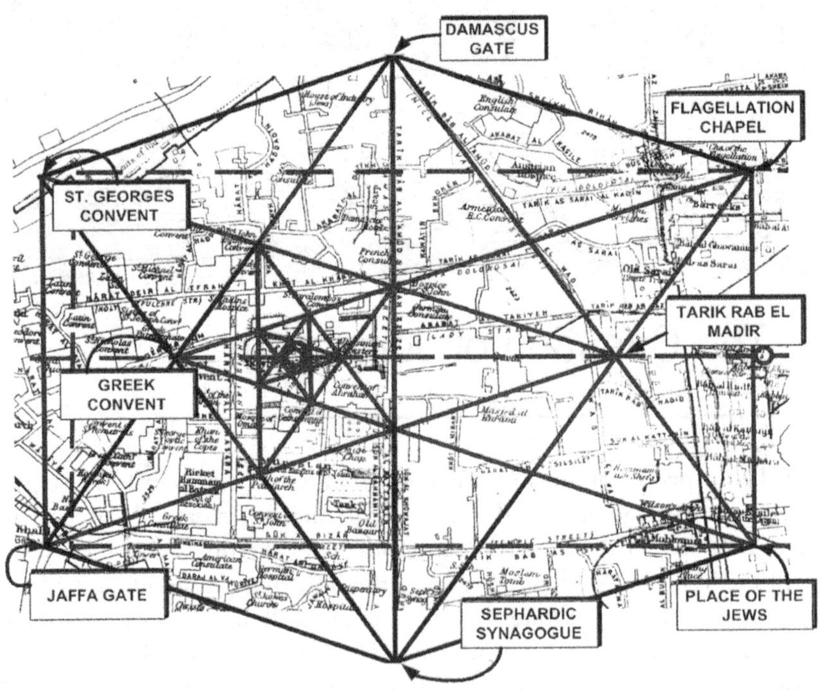

FIG. 56: THE OLD CITY, WITH CHIMNEY LOCATIONS

However, all this took place well before I became aware of the mission the "Family" had assigned to me. When I was told that I had to seek 18 sites, the City of Jerusalem was not one of the ones I had selected. I asked about

Jerusalem in a channeling session with Géèma; and we were told that the work on Jerusalem was being handled by others. Even so, after I had connected the 18 sites, I was repeatedly asked to do some energetic cleansing work on Jerusalem, whose energetic situation may be unstable, attracting negative energies as being a "city of contention" rather than the city of peace it was meant to be (in Hebrew, Ir Shalom means City of Peace).

There was a change in my personal life in the summer of 2010. I met a new partner, Vardit, whom the "Family" said was sent to me at this stage, to help me expand the scope of my work. We began traveling together, forming bonds with other individuals who felt it important to take action in order to heal the condition of the Planet. Strong ties were forged in Spain and Portugal, in addition to the powerful nucleus of students I had built up in France. At the same time, I collated the written material about the mission of the 18 sites; Vardit and I made a joint effort to publish a book in three languages, in order to spread the energy as recommended by the "Family." The "Family" told us through Géèma, how beneficial this book would be for the reader in terms of raising his consciousness.

A few months after we had first met, Vardit and I went for a romantic week-end in Jerusalem. She had found us a charming room at the Scottish Guest House, an ancient building overlooking the Old City. I took this Jerusalem excursion as a sign that I wasn't there simply to enjoy myself, but also to do some work. I brought with me John Michell's book and all the material that I had prepared ten years before.

On the first evening of our stay in Jerusalem, Vardit fell ill; and our plan of taking a walking tour of the Old City the next day was clearly going to have to be scrapped. But the location of the Guest House was absolutely ideal. I could not have chosen a better location for getting on with my work. The Guest House has a garden with some tables and chairs under the shade of tall trees, commanding a view of the Old City. Early the next morning, I sat there with Michell's map spread in front of me. I checked and found that there were chimneys located at each of eight points on the map, mostly at the various gates. I went ahead to activate them. The chimneys were located at:

* Damascus gate

* Tarik Rab el Madir

* Jaffa gate

* Sephardic Synagogue

* Chapel of the Flagellation

* Place of the Jews

* Saint Georges Convent

* Greek Convent

At the start of my work, each of the above locations was at a level of between 2 and 3 million Bovis. After activation, the levels ranged from 12 to 18 million Bovis. It should be noted that the day before our arrival in Jerusalem, the Old City, which is the entire walled area, was at an energy level of 4 million Bovis. After activation, the Old City went up to 29 million Bovis. When I mentally connected the Door to Sirius - at the Seven Hills site - to a central point in the Old City, the level shot up to 56 million Bovis.

The place where I was sitting at the Guest House garden was at a level of 30,000 Bovis the day prior to our arrival. After activation of the points in the Old City, the level went up to 52,000 Bovis. The entire city of Jerusalem - that is spread outside the walls - went from 30,000 to 40,000 Bovis.

The energy of Jerusalem occasionally drops and requires intervention to clear the city of negative energies. This dynamic situation also occurs in urban centers around the world, influenced by social and political fluctuations. Many crises have recently been experienced in the Middle East—Libya, Egypt, and Syria—events mentioned by the "Family," indicating that we are in the middle of sweeping changes.

22... Energetic Voyage

In my wish to share the energetic benefits of the 18 sites, I have organized what I called "An Energetic Voyage," a kind of pilgrimage to Israel for people who are interested in Geobiology. People came from France, Mexico and Denmark to form a small but a lovely group.

We began the outing from the top of Mt. Carmel, which commands a sweeping view of the region. We observed the landscape from the Mukhraka, a site traditionally linked with the Prophet Elijah. One can see as far as Mt. Hermon in the north, the Jordan mountains, the Mediterranean Sea and, toward the south, Netanya.

Our first stop was at the Kursi site. There, we conducted a ceremony in which we charged small crystals with the energy of the large crystal located there, but in the fifth dimension. Each of us took a crystal, as a sort of disk-on-key of high-energy crystalline information, the use of which he or she would be able to use for personal healing, in the future.

At Kibbutz Nir David, the one whose inhabitants live to a ripe old age, we connected with the water element. Hosted by Yael Berkovitz, we sat meditating beside the Asi river. We connected with the memory of the water, with its pure, clean source, as close as possible to where it wells up from the deep in the earth. High-energy sites can arouse vitality, bringing about rejuvenation.

At Megiddo, we performed an experiment on the energy line crossing Israel from Damascus in the direction of Gaza. The Megiddo site regulates the energy of this line, by means of its link to Mt. Tabor. We conducted an experiment there. I asked my friends to limit the flow of energy through the line to just 50% for half an hour. We measured the level on the link prior to blockage (1.1 million Bovis) and after (11 million Bovis.). Sure enough, as soon as the level on the main artery decreased, Megiddo began increasing its output in order to compensate for the weakening of the flow.

We invited our guests to conduct a major purification at Caesarea. The energy site at Caesarea, of course, is a private home, and its level is exceptionally high, but its surroundings have suffered for many years from negative energy. Caesarea was built as one of the most important cities of the Roman conquest era. Caesarea's amphitheater served as a place of execution, with the victims sometimes being thrown to the lions as prey, while the crowd looked on.

Rabbi Akiva, one of the foremost spiritual teachers of that time, was executed there along with hundreds of his disciples. We held a ceremony to release the trapped souls of thousands of individuals. The previously 100% negative energy dissipated to zero.

A special visit was the pilgrimage we made to the Seven Hills site. There we conducted a harmonization ceremony to cover the entire area of Israel, and we prayed for the neutralization of the forces of darkness. Towards evening, one of our French guests, my long-time student Marie-Jane, came to show me a photograph she had taken of the tree where the "Door" to Sirius is located. The camera had captured an astoundingly surprising energy shape, which we hastened to share with the others. In a later channeling about the photograph, the "Family" told us that it showed an energy field that was following us throughout our trip, to protect us.

I would like to focus on the part of the trip that was dedicated to Rujm-el-Hiri, as I understood, from previous communications through Géèma, that this is a place of connection with beings in the fifth dimension, probably

Lemurians. So we went to Rujm with a purpose in mind: to renew the connections that existed in the times of Lemuria and Atlantis.

FIG. 57: THE DOOR TO SIRIUS WITH AMAZING CAMERA SHOT

This place has always been difficult to reach. Having been there twice previously, I had established that Rujm is one of the chakras of our planet. Previously I had done some praying at the highest point of this site, beseeching peace for the region; that was in November 2007.

This time, together with some of the more adventurous members of our group, I decided to enter the site—easier said than done! The entire area was sodden from the constant rains and we had to watch our steps. We arrived at the small river, and, with a great deal of difficulty—but with the help of Elfriede (from France) and José (from Mexico)—I made it across, followed by the others. We continued on to the site and climbed the central tumulus.

Our purpose for being there stemmed from an article I had read by Maia Alaula Kamala, who indicated that Rujm was once called CheRu Agha and was constructed a few years before the fall of Atlantis. She wrote that it was an astro-temple complex, considered one of the most sacred places on Earth in relation to the Heavens. Originally it had been a very active stellar node on the planet, but then its activity dwindled. In the past, Rujm (or CheRu Agha) was connected to Giza, Mecca and Bahrain. A schematic of the connections is shown here, and we see another infinity sign.

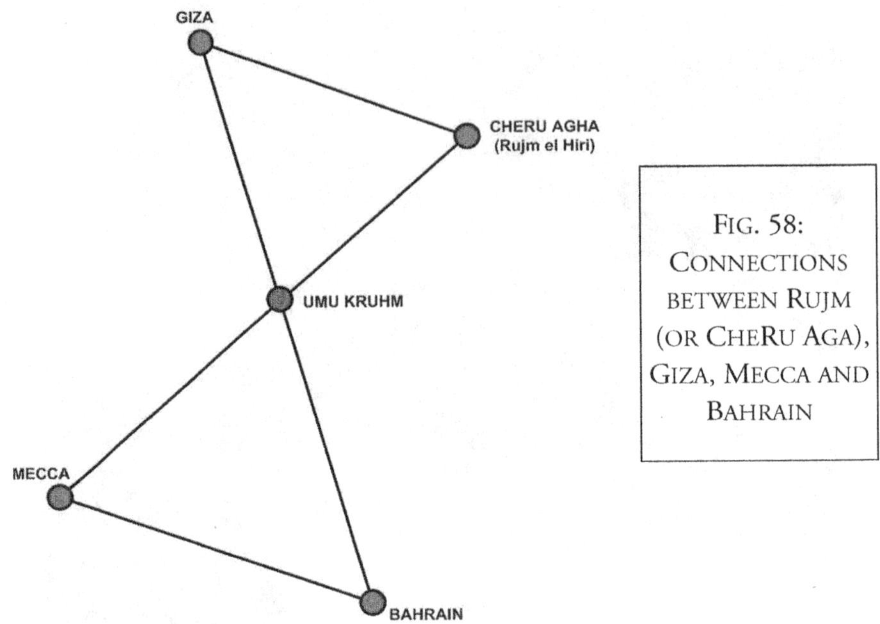

FIG. 58: CONNECTIONS BETWEEN RUJM (OR CHERU AGA), GIZA, MECCA AND BAHRAIN

Standing on the tumulus, I mentally connected Rujm to Giza and to Mecca. I also connected the other points in the hourglass figure, above. Then I proceeded to activate the energy flow among all points.

The four of us, Amelia (our official tour guide), Jose, Elfriede and I then offered up a prayer for peace and to neutralize the dark forces. The next day, my friend Géèma received a message by channeling, part of which said:

"The central point of the site has reached an energetic level never reached in this place."

I measured 2,000 million Bovis for this central point! This is the highest reading I have ever measured. The entire site is at 900 million Bovis.

We received a message from the Family to Géèma and the group, which read:

Hello, our beloved!

Everything that was said is in progress: be confident!

All the souls that make up this group of 27.03.11 are soul-mates including the guide[1] and the driver,[2] strangers to esoteric matters.

This day was blessed as well as those that are to follow, and all of your actions.

Our love is infinite and your actions help to bring you closer to the Family.

You have come a long way to reunite and your reunion continues to unfold during your travel; chance or coincidence? You called this gathering: Energetic Voyage! And for that we shall talk about the VOYAGE.

The trip is to you an act of displacement; for us, VOYAGE is a concept that includes both a vision, movement, and time or age, if you prefer; by analogy, the AGE is a library that is filled with (books) of everything you see and / or feel...the memories.

While present in these magical places, you[3] only see ruins or remains (and often you do not see anything), but you feel the vibration or high energy that summarize past, present and future; to feel the past you rely on history, often deformed; and the present is; to feel the future, you must get rid of your two or three-dimensional logic and this can be done only by the elevation of your consciousness. And that cannot be done without raising your level of energy. This transformation will allow you at first to dream, meditate and get out of your body; as a second stage you will perform moves or quantum leaps thanks to which the time factor will disappear from your priorities and your reality; in a third stage, although later, you'll overcome gravity, transform matter into energy. Then, travel as we now practice, and the related visions, will be done in a no-time space; past, present and future will be one and your free-will shall apply in a HERE AND NOW, including a cosmic vision.

---

1. Amelia —R.B.
2. Georges —R.B.
3. Refers to the entire group —R.B.

We recognize that it is difficult to accept this in your tridimensional grasp of things; it is as if you were described a color that does not exist for you; everything that was said above EXISTS and hereafter we shall give you the formula.

The central point of the site[1] has reached an energy level never attained in this place.

So how should you proceed to travel as we do?

LET GO! BELIEVE THE UNBELIEVABLE!
SEE THE INVISIBLE!
Not easy, we know, but it is the magic formula.

LET GO!

When the group disperses, each participant's energy-level will more than double - and even greater for some.

Each will have targets to reach for the elevation of human consciousness, up to becoming angelic; you are now thousands to do this same work.

We embrace all of you and we create a ring of light that will keep you connected.

Be Blessed,

The Family

---

1. Where we were standing on the tumulus —R.B.

23... The Sky is Not the Limit.

We set up a date to visit Rujm again. This time I was moved by a number of things that followed my work with the 18 sites. A certain message that Géèma had received, played over and over in my mind—the one in which I was told that going back to working at the level of private clients from now on was no longer an option. I should go on working for the benefit of the entire planet. Moreover, the message said: "The Planet and the Universe."

I don't have to tell you the emotional state in which this revelation had put me in. For a long time I have been trying to understand what was expected of me and could not believe the enormity of the responsibility that landed on my shoulders. I wondered if the fact that I have started doing similar work with high energy sites in countries like France and the Ivory Coast means that I will gradually extend this project to include more areas around the world. Was I supposed to find a way to perform harmonization for the entire globe on one single occasion? What?

Finally the answer came. I got a letter from my friend and student Martine. The letter was referring to an interview with a retired Russian cosmonaut, a well known scientist in Russia, Prof. Marina Popovitch. One passage particularly drew my attention:

> Studies found that the planet is surrounded by a vast network of energy, a "fabric" of energy that has a geometric distribution. The geology of the continent…specific geometric patterns. This is known under the term "Sacred Geometry." In addition, in 1958, Professor Bernascki discovered a sort of ring that surrounds the planet and contains an energy field in which are stored "records'" of all forms of life and history of the planet.[1] It was discovered that this energy field is not located on a physical level.…

> We discovered that this field is an emotionally charged etheric fabric. Therefore, it is necessary to control our passions. Each of us has the power to affect this area positively or negatively. All the negativity expressed as hatred and fear has a direct impact on the state of the planet. Earth reacts violently with our thoughts and feelings, and it emits a type of radiation that affects the climate models.…

> In the world everything is interconnected, whatever we do, harmonious or inharmonious, affects the Earth. These negative charges affect humans and are actually more powerful than nuclear energy itself. The planet, as if it were a sick body, reacts with natural antibodies to treat this disorder. Pollution is not caused solely by the production of energy waste. We ourselves are a powerful source of pollution. The world responds to the hate and love."

I got to thinking: If I can remove negativity from people or places, why not from the Earth itself and, in particular, from this ring or band around the Earth? As i did not know exactly how to approach this problem of purifying this ring, I thought that Rujm would be a good place to do this work. I mentioned it to Géèma and I started to think on how to remove this energy from the ring. Once removed, what do I do with it? Where do I send it?

---

1. This may be what some call the Akashic Field. —ed.

A few days later Géèma got a message from the "Family." Of course they knew we were going to Rujm and for what purpose. This was the communication:

> *Let us discuss now the ring mentioned by Popovitch and that we frequently encounter on our plane. In fact, there are two rings. The first receives and stores everything that is positive; thus, when meditation and prayer groups are active, they radiate positive energies. The same happens with humanitarian and compassionate actions. All of these[1] energies arrive at the Gold ring and make it shine.*

> *The second ring is gray. It receives all negative energies; it has a very important function; without it, the chaos on the planet would be greater. But, it happens that right now this ring is saturated; the extra[2] comes back to you and maintains the conflicts and the hate.*

> *We will be able to superimpose these two rings; it shall be up to you to connect them in three points. This will permit the extra energy of the gray ring to pour into the gold ring. Thus the extra negative energies will be eliminated. Thus, the golden ring will grow. The gray ring will become thinner and will turn silver and will, by itself, transmute the negative energies to positive. These extra energies shall be welcomed by the gold ring.*

> *That is what you will have to do. That will cause a big change for your planet.*

Until now I had taught my students that the chimneys were getting positive energy from the cosmos and injecting it throughout the earth, and sending negative energy from the earth to the cosmos.

I have two new suppositions based on the new facts about the rings:

- If we influence the universe so much, I suppose that the negative energy is sent to the gray ring and not to the cosmos.

- In addition, I suppose that the chimneys receive positive energy from the gold ring.

---

1. Positive—R.B.
2. Negative energy—R.B.

I see the Earth as an integrated system, that is looped on itself. I don't think that the rest of the universe should be our trash can. When I posed the question to the "Family," I received confirmation of my suppositions.

On the date planned (August 16, 2011), Vardit, Géèma and I drove to Rujm. We had prepared ourselves for crossing the river by wearing new rubber boots and holding on to a walking stick, which helped us cross successful. After a somewhat difficult walk on the rocky terrain, we formed a circle at the side of the tumulus and set up a compass in the center.

Géèma said to us that the "Family" joined us and that they were moving the rings one upon the other. When that was done, they signaled through Géèma, that we could start concentrating on making the respective connections between the two rings. We have put our minds together and did what was required of us.

Immediately after completion, Géèma got this feedback for us:

You are at the meeting for this great job we asked you to do. As we promised, we are all here to help you and to protect you.

Actually the activation of the two rings in their new configuration is taking place, and that will take a few days to complete. Don't be surprised if there will be events that you are familiar with: the Earth has slightly shaken some time ago; the sea rose two meters[1] for some hours.

Be ready for other events, geophysical as well as social. The [2]energy that is being withdrawn from the Earth is going to cause some great political and governmental changes....

The job is done. Let the Peace come.

---

1. 6.5 ft
2. Negative —R.B.

The Second Volume in the Series

*M*ission: *Mother Earth–No Task is Too Big* is the second volume in the series "Between the Earth and the Skies," to be published in 2014.

Having completed the different Israeli sites, I found myself faced with the new challenges that the "Family" had placed in front of me:

To continue to work for the good of the entire Planet.

During 2011 through 2013, some additional projects were undertaken with the help of my students in France, Spain and Israel. Together we worked on high-energy sites and atomic reactors both in France and in Spain. I undertook the task of neutralizing the negative energies produced by reactors in Japan and managed to raise that country's energy level to a new high.

In February 2012, I started anew, concentrating on the Cosmic Serpent Line[1] and extending this line on both sides of the original section passing through Israel, and unblocking it along its global path.

Getting information from my friends in Paris, I started to work on the critically low-energy-level countries around the world. Once I increased the energy of each country, I tied it into the Cosmic Serpent Line.

In addition, I addressed various constellations. Indeed, if Sirius is connected to the Earth, as I have shown in this first volume of the *Between the Earth and the Skies* series, then why not other portals? With this train of thought, specific

---

1. This is the high-energy line passing through Mount Tabor and running around the Earth. Refer to Chapter 15 on page 89.

connecting locations on the planet were identified for the Pleiades, Orion and Andromeda constellations. These portals were located, activated and connected, in time, to the Cosmic Serpent Line. I was told that I need to look for and connect six more constellations. Two of these—Cassopeia and Proxima Centauri—are next.

As a final, large project, and again with the help of my students, we were able to slow down the outpouring of negative entities from the center of the Earth and to channel these into the Cosmic Serpent Line for transmutation into positive entities. This work was done using 33 volcanoes, selected globally, each configured in a very special and interesting way.

The next project in line of massive impact—correcting the negative energies around the atomic reactors in the USA—will be completed during 2014, and the results of that project will be included in book two of the series.

Finally, my students in Spain—a group I am particularly fond of—have started a *huge* project, after I sought guidance on how to combine Geobiology with the Mayan calendar. This question has been answered, and work is underway. Some refer to the Mayan calendar as Tzolk'in. This project is going to make a big impact with 20 sectors on Planet Earth, each sector having 13 stars of seven chimneys each.

—Richard Benishai

October 2013

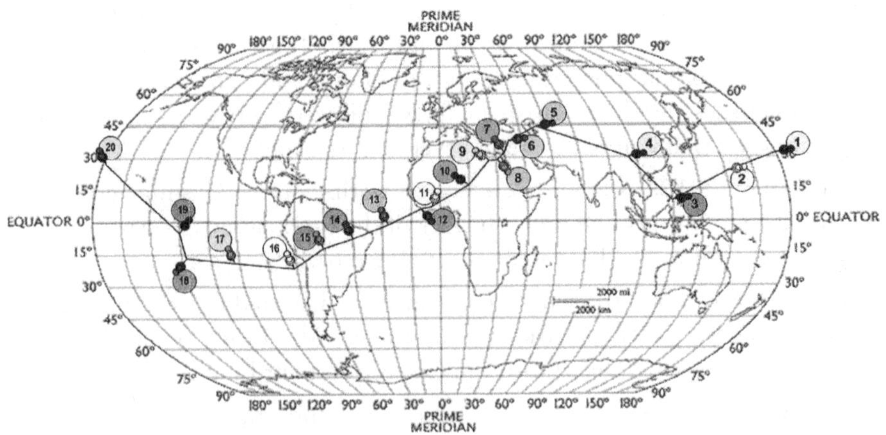

FIG. 59: THE COSMIC SERPENT LINE

About the Author

Richard Benishai had an unusual beginning. He was born in Algeria in 1943 and just as his mother went into labor, German planes started bombing his town. Luckily the family survived. In 1956, as Algeria's War of Independence began, his parents decided to move the family to the United States when the Jewish population became undermined.

After attending college for a year, he knew that he didn't want to settle down and joined the US military where he served three years as a communications and electronics technician. This led to a job with Philco-Ford in the communications domain, which allowed him to see the world while solving technical problems.

During his 4th business trip to Israel, he met a woman who would become his wife. At the age of 31, he took the bold step to immigrate to Israel and begin a new life. They subsequently had four sons.

After six years of working at a high-tech firm, he became self-employed. It was also at this time where he contracted a violent headache that lasted several days. After receiving hands-on treatment, the pain went away. To him, it was a miracle and an occurrence that opened his mind.

While attending a four-day seminar with Drunvalo Melchizedek, he was introduced to Geobiology and he received a clear understanding that this was his path. To become adept in the field, he studied in the United States and France.

Fate has brought him together with people and situations in which he could prove his abilities in the fields of energy, healing, the paranormal and bioenergy. Since 2000, Richard has spent much of his time in study and research in these areas. He has co-authored publications related to geobiology and has intervened for peace in countries such as the USA, the Ivory Coast, Israel, Spain, Portugal and France.

Presently he is working on a global level, increasing the energy level of the planet, country-by-country. He still lives in Israel

Made in the USA
Monee, IL
07 July 2026